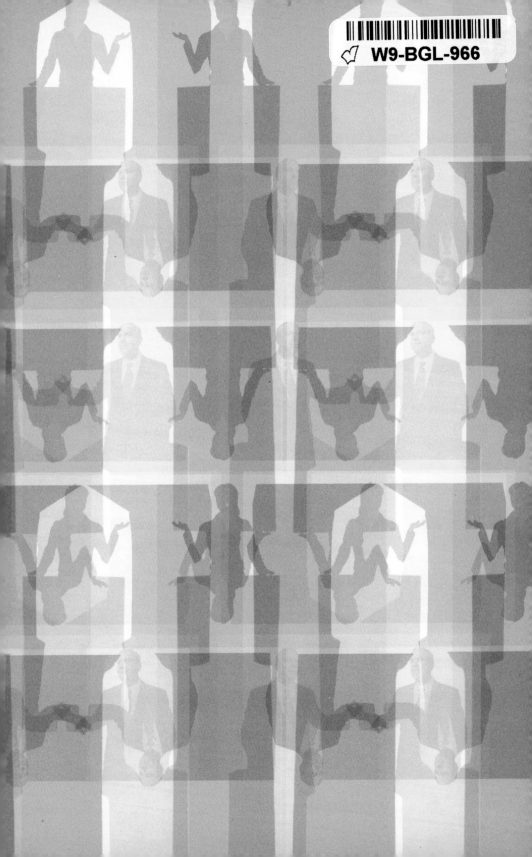

W9-BGL-966

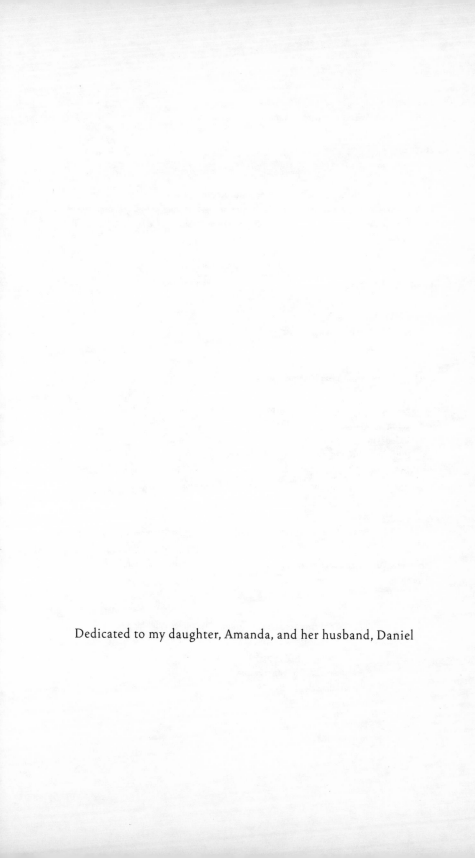

Dedicated to my daughter, Amanda, and her husband, Daniel

Published by Clearbridge Publishing
A division of the Science of Strategy Institute

FIRST EDITION
Copyright 2006 Gary Gagliardi

All rights reserved. No part of this book may be reproduced or transmitted in any part or by any means, electronic or mechanical, including photocopying, recording, or by any information storage and retrieval system, without the written permission of the Publisher, except where permitted by law.

The Science of Strategy Institute, Clearbridge Publishing and its logo are the trademarks of Clearbridge Publishing.

Printed in China.
Interior and cover graphic design by Gary Gagliardi.

Publisher's Cataloging-in-Publication Data

   Making money by speaking — the spokesperson strategy / Gary Gagliardi.
   p. 192 cm. 23
   Includes introduction to basic competitive philosophy of Sun Tzu
   ISBN 978-1929194-41-4
   1. Public speaking 2. New business enterprise—U.S. 3. Home-based business. 4. Small business—U.S. I. Gagliardi, Gary 1951–. II. Making money by speaking.
HD62.5 2002
658.11 —dc21

                          Library of Congress Catalog Card Number: 2006902144

Clearbridge Publishing's books may be purchased for business, for any promotional use, or for special sales. Please contact:

The Science of Strategy Institute: Clearbridge Publishing
PO Box 33772, Seattle, WA 98133
Phone: (206)533-9357 Fax: (206)546-9756
www.scienceofstrategy.com
info@clearbridge.com

MAKING
MONEY BY
SPEAKING

**The
Spokesperson
Strategy
for Marketing
Your Expertise**

Award Recognition for Recent Books by Gary Gagliardi

The Golden Key to Strategy

Psychology/Self-Help
Ben Franklin
Book Award
2006 - Winner

The Art of War Plus The Ancient Chinese Revealed

Multicultural Nonfiction
Independent Publishers
Book Award
2003 - Winner

The Art of Marketing

Business
Ben Franklin
Book Award
2004 - Finalist

Strategy Against Terror

Philosophy
Foreword Magazine
Book of the Year
2005 - Finalist

The Warrior's Apprentice

Youth Nonfiction
Independent Publishers
Book Award
2006 - Semi-Finalist

Strategy for Sales Managers

Business
Independent Publishers
Book Award
2006 - Semi-Finalist

The Warrior Class: 306 Lessons in Strategy

Self-Help
Foreword Magazine
Book of the Year
2005 - Finalist

The Art of War Plus Its Amazing Secrets

Multicultural Nonfiction
Independent Publishers
Book Award
2005 - Finalist

Making
MONEY BY
SPEAKING

The Spokesperson Strategy for Marketing Your Expertise

by Gary Gagliardi

Clearbridge Publishing

The Science of Strategy Institute
www.ScienceOfStrategy.com

Book Programs
Library Memberships
Book Clubs
Books and Audios

On-line Training Programs
The Warrior Class
The Strategy School

Academy of Strategy
On-line Training
The Academy Library
Mentoring on Life Strategy

Strategy Institute Seminars
A Worldwide Network of Trainers
Internal Corporate Licensing

Contents

Making Money by Speaking
The Spokesperson Strategy for Marketing Your Expertise

Chapter 1

Success
From Speaking

The Spokesperson Strategy:
From Nobody to Somebody

Success is easy if you speak out. Forget about public speaking for a moment and think about becoming a spokesperson. A spokesperson is a champion for a cause, an organization, a product, or a point of view. By getting heard you can convince others to work with you or your organization, to buy your products, to join your cause, or to follow your lead. A spokesperson is not a salesperson but a invaluable expert at exciting audiences about his or her ideas.

Becoming a spokesperson is the easiest path to success. Most people are afraid of public speaking. That is why there are so many opportunities to speak. But there is an easy formula for eliminating the fear so you can enjoy these opportunities.

Making money by speaking is about rewards. No matter how hard you work, you will never be well rewarded for your efforts unless you learn to speak up for yourself. If you don't speak up, all the thousands of people who could hear about you won't. If you don't speak up for yourself, no one else can.

Does it seem to you that the same people always dominate the conversation? Does it seem like these people always get more than their share of the rewards and recognition?

Simply by speaking out you redefine your place in the world. Speaking is the only true shortcut to success.

You don't have to be obnoxious, egotistical, or aggressive to speak up for yourself. The power of the spokesperson strategy is that it enables you to champion ideas for the good of your audience. In return, you move yourself from the background where you are easily ignored, to the front of the room, where the rewards are.

When you try to stand up for yourself, do you tend to get into fights instead of get your point across? When you try to make your point, do you get nervous and frustrated?

Our instinctual reactions to a challenge are flight or fight. Without training, we all naturally get frightened or angry. When you choose not to stand up for yourself, your adrenaline starts pumping and—if you don't know how to channel that energy—your emotions take control.

When you are trained in being a spokesperson, you know how to channel your emotions. When you channel your energy into speaking, you will move up in your career and enhance people's opinion of you. Becoming a passionate spokesperson is the easiest way to change the way you feel about yourself and the way others see you.

Of course, by speaking, you can also make a fool of yourself, which is why it scares people. Most people do not know what they should say, how they should say it, or whom they should say it to. But these are skills you can develop easily. The eight steps in this book take the fear and mystery out of speaking.

If you don't speak up for yourself, nobody else will. If you do speak up, everyone will notice and listen to you.

In this chapter, you learn why becoming a speaker is the easiest route to success.

In the next chapter, you learn how to plug your story in to your audience's passions.

In the third chapter, you learn how easy it is to develop an area of expertise and a topic that you can champion.

In the fourth chapter, you learn how to package your ideas into assets that your audience can use.

In the fifth chapter, you learn the key steps to accessing the thousands of great opportunities for speakers.

In the sixth chapter, you learn how to influence others through persuasive presentations.

In the seventh chapter, you learn the nuts and bolts of finding opportunities and preparing yourself to speak.

In the eighth chapter, you learn how to create great events that produce the best results.

In the final chapter, we will give you access to some invaluable tools to help you start right away.

The most successful people aren't those who know the most or work the hardest. Successful people find and use opportunities to influence others. By becoming a speaker and spokesperson, you become comfortable with people. You establish yourself as an expert. You get visibility in the world, and you increase the value of everything you have to offer.

Most people are terribly afraid of speaking. Because they never learn to speak in public, they never earn the credibility they need to make themselves heard in any aspect of their lives. This is exactly why the spokesperson strategy represents such a

great opportunity. It offers a safe, painless way
to turn yourself into a powerful, persuasive
personality in a few easy steps.

The Spokesperson Strategy

The best strategy that I have found for transforming an ordinary life into an extraordinary one is speaking.

As one of the world's leading authorities
on strategy, I have written a number of award-
winning books and trained the world's leading
organizations. Over many years of working
with thousands of people, I began to notice that those who
were the most successful had one thing in common. They were
able to communicate their strategy to others.

Pondering this fact, I realized why speaking is so important and why it was in my own best interest to teach people its
secrets. Strategy teaches that you cannot advance your position
by force. You need a leverage point. Becoming a spokesperson
provides that leverage. The entire process of speaking teaches
you how to pursue success, not by taking big, risky leaps, but
by taking small, safe, and certain steps.

No matter what your current position, your success demands that you package, promote, and sell yourself. Speaking
is at once the most powerful form of promotion and the easiest
and least expensive. Packaging yourself as a spokesperson
makes it easy for you to speak out.

If you follow this path, you will become more successful.
You will then need to learn more about the more advanced
forms of strategy that our organization teaches. You might
even join our organization so we can help you in your role as a
spokesperson. People who are stuck in the same place have a
limited need for our services. Over the long term, my goal is to

I made millions by speaking before I was paid a dime in speaking fees. Making money is easy when you speak out.

get everyone in the world using the principles of strategy so that we can all make better decisions every day and create a better world.

The Path for Everyone

This book is about using speaking to make yourself successful. It is not about becoming a professional speaker and supporting yourself with speaking fees. It is about becoming a spokesperson and an advocate. Many books claim that you can make millions from public speaking, but for most people, huge speaking fees are pie in the sky. Unless you are a celebrity, you do not get paid huge sums for speaking. You can, however, become richly rewarded for becoming a passionate spokesperson.

Speaking is a brilliant way to promote yourself, a great way to promote your business, and the most powerful way to sell products. In other words, becoming a passionate advocate makes you money even when you are not getting paid to speak.

I made millions by speaking before I ever got paid a dime in speaking fees. I made money by speaking out within my company to get myself pay raises and promotions. I made money by getting commissions from sales that I won by being a spokesperson for my company. I made money by promoting my software business and making it one of the Inc. 500 fastest-growing privately held companies in America. Finally, I made millions by speaking to investors and selling my company.

In my research for this book, I read all the get-rich-quick-by-speaking books. Written by professional speakers, speaker bureau owners, or speaker trainers, they all have the same flaw. Their approach to speaking won't work for the average person.

Don't get me wrong—every book I read had some good ideas. I've applied many of those ideas to the lessons in this book. But the approach they teach is not based on sound strategy. Building a business as a speaker requires hard work and a lot of luck.

Afraid of speaking? Everyone is. This fact is why becoming a spokesperson has become the world's greatest opportunity.

This approach is more realistic. It isn't about becoming a celebrity. Becoming a spokesperson is a marketing strategy. You use it to create a dominant position for yourself within your organization. You use it to create a dominant position for your organization within the larger marketplace.

My job isn't to motivate you to try the impossible. It is just the opposite. I want you to stop wasting your time doing what is really difficult. Strategy is about finding the easy way. The point of this book is that speaking as a spokesperson is a natural shortcut to success.

The Fear of Speaking Is Good

Why does this huge opportunity exist? Strategy teaches that opportunities exist because people leave you openings. Fear creates the many openings for speakers.

If you are like most people, you are afraid of public speaking. It is the most common fear in the world. The fact that most people are afraid of public speaking is why embracing it is such a great strategy. Strategy teaches that you cannot be successful doing what everyone else is doing. You have to find an opening that everyone else has overlooked or avoided.

The fear of speaking means that a specific type of opportunity exists in every community, organization, and industry.

A spokesperson is a champion for a valuable point of view. Every organization and cause is looking for a spokesperson.

This is the opening for good spokespeople. A spokesperson isn't a salesperson. A spokesperson is someone who talks on a topic that people find interesting, and by speaking promotes a point of view that audiences find valuable.

If you work in a small company, your company probably doesn't have a good spokesperson within its community. If you work in a large organization, your department probably doesn't have a good spokesperson within the larger corporation. In both cases, your organization probably needs better spokespeople within its industry or within its customers' or clients' industries.

These openings for good spokespeople are tremendous opportunities. It is easy to become a good spokesperson. It is easy to find a cause, product, or company to become a spokesperson for. By becoming a spokesperson, you automatically raise the value of your opinion. You make yourself more visible and valuable in your organization and in your marketplace.

These dominant positions are waiting for you for one reason: most people, including the best experts and the best managers, who should be spokespeople are afraid of speaking. These opportunities for spokespeople wouldn't exist if they weren't.

This is why the world's most successful people are not necessarily the most talented. They aren't the best managers, the best salespeople, the best accountants, or the best doctors, lawyers, or architects. They also aren't necessarily the bravest about speaking.

The fear of speaking is not irrational. Our fear of the unknown is nature's safety device. Most people don't know the recipe for speaking. When they speak out, the results are often disastrous. Mark Twain said, "Better to keep your mouth closed and be thought a fool than to open it and remove all doubt." I have seen highly paid executives embarrass themselves because they didn't know the rules for speaking.

Fear goes away when you get into speaking gradually so that you always know what to say and how to say it.

The antidote to fear is experience. Experience outmaneuvers fear. Each chapter in this book helps you build your experience gradually, one painless step at a time. Every step is so small that fear isn't an issue. By the time you are facing serious audiences, you will have the experience and confidence to know exactly what to do.

It Isn't About Being Brilliant

It is about making money, earning respect, and becoming more and more effective in your life. Your path to success starts with a simple fact: those who get the credit and make money are those who stand up to talk. Let me prove this to you.

Have you ever heard of Richard Bandler? Probably not. Richard Bandler invented a training system called neural linguistic programming (NLP). If you've heard of NLP, it isn't because of Mr. Bandler. It is because of Tony Robbins.

You probably have heard of Tony Robbins. He is one of the best-known professional spokespeople in the world. He built a huge financial empire. He built his financial empire on NLP, but he didn't invent it; Richard Bandler did.

Tony Robbins gets the credit for neural linguistic programming for one reason: he spoke about it. This book explains why Tony Robbins is well known and very wealthy while you have never heard of Richard Bandler. Tony Robbins has money, pow-

Some experts make their topic hard and some make it easy. Which type of experts make the money and which don't?

er, and prestige because he became a spokesperson, while Richard Bandler, the original expert, has his anonymity.

The truth is that you don't have to be brilliant to be successful. You don't have to be the most expert. Bandler was a true expert in psychology. He started a new discipline, wrote books, and even started a school. This extreme expertise did not matter.

What do you need to become successful? What do you do to become a great spokesperson? How was Tony Robbins different from Richard Bandler? Tony Robbins knew the secrets of speaking—secrets that you are going to learn from this book.

I have taught tens of thousands of people the secrets to strategy. After hearing me speak or reading one of my books, no one says, "This is really hard." Instead, what I usually hear is, "This is so easy that I should have thought of it myself."

Strategy is much more complicated than speaking. The secrets to becoming a spokesperson are relatively simple once you know them. My job is to make it easy.

Given the formulas in this book, you can easily turn whatever you find valuable—your own ideas or other people's ideas—into a great reputation and financial security. You don't have to have a special ability. You don't have to be born a genius. You don't even need a great deal of courage. You just need to follow the lessons that have been laid out for you here.

A Simple System

This book adapts the methods of the world's most successful speakers into a process that anyone can use to become a passionate spokesperson. This process takes you one step at a time to a complete understanding of how you can use speaking to make yourself more successful.

Follow these eight steps and you will become a speaker, a spokesperson, and an expert, especially at making money.

The chapters of this book take you through a series of processes. Each process develops your money-making ability as a speaker in a different way. You master each process gradually with practice. It is easy to get started. You don't have to master any one area before going on to the next. In the end, you make progress in each of these areas by getting more and more experience speaking. All these areas of skill become more polished over time.

You learn the following:

1. Understanding the leverage of speaking.

Simply by reading this chapter, you will see the value of speaking in a different way. However, you will not really understand how speaking changes you and changes your position until you actually start speaking in public.

2. Plugging in to your audience's interests.

To connect with your audience you have to know their interests and how their world is changing. Being passionate about your topic is not enough. Your job is to get your audience to take action. You can only do that by leveraging their emotions.

3. Developing an area of expertise.

Your current situation is the basis for developing a unique area of expertise. Developing your expertise is easier than you think. It is also the path to finding the right audiences.

A great speaker is not a technician. The true expertise of a

Speaking makes it possible to gradually advance in your position over time in many dimensions at once.

speaker is making a little practical knowledge new for an audience. You only have to know a little more than your audience does to bring them a great deal of value.

4. Creating assets that can make you money.

Speaking is a way to market your expertise, but selling your time is the least profitable way of making money. You need an asset, a product that allows you to deliver value to your audience without consuming your precious time. Before you speak, you have to have a product. You may already have that product; if not we will show you how to create it.

5. Finding better and better opportunities to speak.

There are millions of speaking opportunities every year. What opportunity is best for you depends on what stage you are at in developing your speaking ability. At first, you choose the safest speaking venues to develop your skills. As time goes on, you move up to larger and more valuable venues.

6. Building persuasive presentations.

If you study the speeches of the most successful professional speakers, you will discover that they all use a very similar format. This format combines the most powerful elements of persuasion into a specific structure designed to get a commitment to action from the audience. All you need to do is use this format as a template for your basic presentations.

7. Managing and growing your speaking operation.

Speaking opens the door for making money, but you still have work to do. You need a little organization to maximize your orders, deliver the goods, and keep customers coming back for more.

8. Creating a good event from start to finish.

You are going to get opportunities to speak. When you do, preparation beforehand and follow-through afterward are critical to your success. Getting the most out of a speaking event requires more than making a great presentation. It requires knowing how to handle the details that result in making you money.

9. Getting started right away.

We make it easy.

> *No one starts out to become a public speaker. However, the path to success leads through speaking for logical reasons.*

My Personal Story

Your success matters to me because it has become my personal mission to teach good strategy. I was an aimless, insecure college dropout when I learned the power of the spokesperson strategy firsthand. I fell into the role one small step at a time. I started in sales, talking to customers one-on-one. As I moved to larger customers, I began giving presentations to committees. Eventually, I was giving those presentations to larger and larger groups. Eventually I was presenting to audiences of thousands.

As I learned the secrets of presentation, I began talking less and less about my product and more and more about topics that sold my products indirectly. I began to talk more about my personal interests, specifically, Sun Tzu's *The Art of War.* Though my product was software, my presentations explained the original principles of strategy, using its logic to attract people to my products.

At first I didn't know why it was working, but after I began speaking, our software company became one of the fastest-

It seems strange, but it is easier to become a successful writer by speaking out than it is by simply writing.

growing (and most profitable) companies in America. Our success gave me more opportunities to speak to larger and larger audiences.

Speaking made me into an expert. Speaking gave me topics for writing articles. Speaking gave me the credibility to get those articles published. The articles gave us more publicity. Speaking and writing articles became a machine for publicity. I wasn't a writer or a speaker, but by speaking and writing, I was making a lot of money despite not being paid a dime in speaking fees.

At first I was just selling my time consulting and the time of my associates. As we grew, we discovered more profitable products to sell. Eventually I sold the ultimate product: my software company itself.

Through this whole process, I never saw myself as a speaker or a spokesperson. I saw myself as a businessperson. After selling my software company, I was financially independent, but people kept inviting me to speak all over the world.

People don't seek me out because I am a great orator. Nobody has ever accused me of having a powerful personality or a smooth speaking style, or being able to tell a joke well. I never worried about any of that and neither should you. Why do people seek me out to speak? For the same reason they will seek you out.

People invite regular people to speak because we know a little something they are curious to learn. They keep inviting us to speak because our little bit of knowledge gets more interesting the more we speak. Over the last couple of decades I have spoken on dozens of topics, but all those topics are based on the same core concepts of strategy. When you understand a few core principles, you can apply them over and over again to a wide variety of topics.

I originally developed the techniques in this book to train the speakers for the Science of Strategy Institute.

The key to your success will be the same as the key to my success. You must know how to organize your speeches so that at the end of your presentations people are more curious than ever about learning more from you.

Since I have only a limited amount of time to devote to speaking, I started licensing others to use my presentation materials. This led to the Science of Strategy Institute, an international organization of strategic trainers.

As our organization grew, I began researching what made speakers and trainers successful. Our trainers came from a variety of backgrounds. They taught strategy in a variety of different industries and for different purposes. I started going to presentations by successful trainers in a variety of areas to pick up as many ideas as I could about how to help them.

In doing this research, I realized that there was a formula in the way the most successful speakers operated. Because many aspects of their approach was nonintuitive, I began researching the psychology of influence so that I could understand it. The result was the first version of this book, which was developed to train our trainers in the fine art of presentation and persuasion.

You can duplicate my success, the success of the world's best presenters, and the success of our trainers by following the simple steps in this book. The approach is timeless, universal, and proven. You will find its ideas exciting and stimulating as you are introduced to them.

Successful speakers can become celebrities, but you don't have to be a celebrity to be a success at speaking.

Making the Money

If you follow the processes in this book, you will immediately start making more money than you are making now. You will not make money from your speaking fees. Spokespeople make money from offering a point of view that wins people over. You win audiences over to wanting to work with you and support you.

That is why we say that speaking isn't a business; it is the way of doing business.

Money-making speaking engagements are designed for one purpose and one purpose only: to get people excited enough to take the next step. To do this, you have to think about speaking in a different way. You don't speak only to educate people. You approach the whole process as a simple exercise in persuasion.

The biggest mistake I have made—and still make—in speaking is that I put too much information into my presentations. When it comes to getting people excited, less is usually more. People retain only 10 percent of what they hear. You need to gear your presentation not to what you know but to what an audience can use to make a decision. This requires less information and more good technique than most people realize.

Money-making speaking presentations are built around knowing what you are promoting. This may lead you to think that a good speech is a sales pitch. This is both very right and very wrong. In a good presentation, the audience never feels as though it is being sold. The key to making money by speaking is building your presentation so that it interests and excites your audience about your topic. It leaves them at a fever pitch, wanting to know more. As a service, it ends by telling them how they can get more.

> *Making money is easy and natural when you know the right process for putting your message in front of others.*

A Few Final Thoughts on Success

You must start where you are. You start speaking as a spokesperson for what you already know and do. It might be any aspect of the industry you are in, the work you perform, or interests you have. All are potentially the basis for making money, but you must take advantage of the opportunities that you have to speak up.

It doesn't matter if you are afraid to speak in public. It doesn't matter if you are afraid to speak to your boss. If you follow the easy steps laid out in this book, your fear won't stop you. It won't even slow you down.

After reading just this first chapter, you should already be seeing your position in a new light. You are already thinking about what you could become instead of what you are, about becoming a spokesperson for the work you do instead of just a worker who does it. The next step is getting in touch with your passion. That passion is there, just waiting to be tapped.

—CHAPTER 2—
PASSION
FOR AN AUDIENCE

Your Positioning Strategy:
From Boring to Soaring

To be successful, you have to start from where you are with your life story. When speaking, you are more concerned about connecting with your audience's passions than finding your own. You do not need a sparkling personality or a brilliant topic to become an influential spokesperson. What makes you interesting is not determined by who you are or what you know or even the cause you champion. What makes you interesting to audiences is your ability to touch their emotions.

Being a spokesperson is not about how great you are or how great your organization is. It is not about how great your product is or how great your cause is. Speaking is about how you can make your audience great. Before you can become a spokesperson for any organization, product, cause, or concept, you must become a champion for your audience. This chapter teaches you how to see your world and your life from a perspective that makes you interesting to audiences.

The Audience's Perspective

What do audiences care about? What do people care about? Each group has its own perspective. We all have hearts, but different groups are interested in different aspects of the human heart. A group of cardiologists is interested in technology that can help them do their jobs. A group of heart attack victims is interested in knowing how to survive their disease. A group of honeymooners is interested in what happens once they have found their hearts' desires.

The road to passion doesn't start with what you care about but with understanding what others care about.

Your value to audiences is not based on any deep, detailed technical knowledge. It is based on your understanding their particular situation. Most audiences are not interested in technical information beyond the minimum they need to know. They are interested in practical information that is relevant to their hopes and fears.

Audiences are interested in ideas and information they can use. The more technical the information, the smaller the audience there is for it. The successful spokesperson takes a little technical knowledge and puts it into a context that regular people can apply to their everyday problems. This is a relatively easy task but one that too few people are willing to perform. Remember Richard Bandler and Tony Robbins? Richard Bandler had the technical knowledge. Tony Robbins made the critical connection to that knowledge. Which was the most valuable?

What should you be a spokesperson for? First, you should be a spokesperson for your audience. Start by understanding your connection to the audience and what your life itself can mean to them. Your actual topic is secondary. Your topic will evolve,

but your real life will always be the basis for your life story. Your first job is connecting your life story with your audience's interests.

Becoming a successful spokesperson is a matter of appealing to the mass of people most experts are neglecting.

Don't expect your friends and relatives to help you in this process. None of us are interesting to those who know us well. We only become interesting when we get in front of an audience to whom we can become the expert from afar. The more you speak to different groups of people, the more you learn what audiences are interested in and how to serve them.

Your Boring, Exciting Life Thus Far

The path to your success can only start from where you are. By definition, where you start in this process will be very different from where you end. You will find your starting point in your current life and past experiences. Your experience thus far always offers you the first easy steps on the path to success if you know how to look for them.

There is an exciting way to see your life experiences. There is also a boring way to see your life. Most people get stuck seeing their lives in the boring way.

An infinite number of details make your life unique. What do you do for a living? What education do you have? Where do you live? What jobs and positions have you held? What experiences have affected you the most? The list goes on and on. These details are great source material, but, by themselves, the details of your life aren't interesting to an audience.

What interests people? Patterns are exciting. Pattern recognition is hard wired into our human brains. What makes your life relevant to other people is the pattern that it follows. Audiences find the patterns of your life interesting because they can relate them to the patterns in their lives. Audiences care about your life story because, told correctly, it gives them new perspective on their own lives.

> *Everyone has a story. The young can connect people to what is new. Older people can connect them to what lasts.*

The Key Points of Connection

What parts of your experiences can be the most helpful to audiences? While you can and should ask this question for each audience you address, you start by thinking about all audiences in general. How do you find a pattern in your life story?

You need only five key issues to connect to the passions of your audience. These connection points are: 1) our common ground of shared needs, 2) our changing times, 3) our character, 4) the skills we can share, and 5) our mutual goals.

Why are these five elements so important? Speaking is storytelling. All good storytelling comes down to answering the same basic questions. The patterns that we look for in stories resolve the five basic questions—where, when, who, what, and why. The common ground, the changing times, our character, our skills, and our goals answer these questions. These are your connection points with your audience.

Your first responsibility as a spokesperson is to get people to act. Emotions overcome the inertia that prevents action. To get an audience to act, you must connect with their emotions. Each of these five elements touches your audience's emotions.

An audience relates to your story by connecting it to their

P
A
S
S
I
O
N

Becoming a spokesperson forces you to think about your relationship with audiences and how you can help them.

own situation. You have a where, when, who, what, and why in your life story. Everyone in your audience also has a where, when, who, what, and why in their life story as well. Your success comes from connecting the dots.

Where Is the Need?

Think of yourself as a spokesperson for your audiences' needs. Each individual has his or her own needs, but audiences are special. They are drawn together because they share a need, a skill, or a goal. In other words, they share common ground. All emotional bonds arise from sharing common ground.

You build your presentations on the foundation of this common ground. You don't need to worry about the individual concerns of every audience member. You concentrate on one or more shared needs that bring them together. Even though the people in your audience come from very different places, they come together because they have something in common.

For example, I recently spoke to a group of corporate travel buyers who were invited to a conference by Hyatt Hotels. Corporate travel buyers and their Hyatt hosts came to the conference from two different places, but both came together out of their common need to deepen their knowledge of one another and relationships with each other.

Understanding the needs of audiences is the basis of making money by speaking. Remember how we said that strategy defines an opportunity as an opening? Your audience's unmet needs are your opportunity. Their common needs are your opportunity to provide them value and get rewarded for it.

When you initially plan on speaking to a general audience, you can address only the most generic forms of common needs. The more you focus on a specific type of audience and a specific type of need, the more powerful your presentations become. You will have many different audiences over the years. Each audience will offer its own common ground. Over time, you will get better and better at finding and more profitably targeting each audience's needs.

Every experience you have had potentially defines a place where you can connect with an audience's interests.

When Is the Change?

You must also be a spokesperson for the future. As humans, we cannot know our future, but we cannot help but react emotionally to it. Our hopes and fears are all tied up with how our world is changing and how those changes might affect us. Our emotions continuously swing between the extremes of excitement and boredom, hope and fear, as we react to change.

The emotions of your audience are determined by the changes they are facing. Most of your audience's emotions are based on what is happening outside the room as you speak. Over the years, I have spoken to audiences whose industries were fading, whose businesses were booming, and whose worlds were changing so quickly they didn't know what to think. Each audience looks at the passage of time differently.

Many speakers mistakenly think that they can control the emotions of their audience. It is more accurate to say that good speakers leverage the emotions of their audience. They do not create those feelings. Audiences are not puppets. What happens to them in the room is not as important as the real changes that

affect their lives outside the room.

Your audience is always concerned about what is changing. Change is the source of all danger and opportunity.

You use the reality of change to motivate audiences. You use the emotions that people already have. Once you learn what changes are affecting your audience, you know what emotional buttons you can push. You can transform a chilly reception into a warm one by making your presentation address change.

Your approach must draw upon the changes the audience is going through. It must connect with their feelings about their changing situation. You use the hopes and fears of your audience as part of your story. You play upon their emotions. You connect with the strong emotions that already exist. You start with what they are already feeling. You can then leverage those emotions to get the response you desire.

Who Is Your Character?

You must also be a spokesperson for yourself. No matter what your topic, your life is part of it. Think of your life as if you were a character in a story. Your life story describes the development of your character. Don't plumb your psychological depths. Your audience only cares about five characteristics in your personality: your caring, your intelligence, your trustworthiness, your self-discipline, and your courage. These five characteristics alone are the focus of your story.

All good stories follow the same pattern. You start with your faults and weaknesses. You come to a point of decision and transformation. You end as a better character for your trials. The physical changes in your life only reflect the internal changes in your character.

Your initial fault or weakness can be a lack of caring, intelligence, trustworthiness, self-discipline, or courage, but it can also be an excess of these qualities. Too much caring leads to oversensitivity, too much intelligence to overanalysis, too much trustworthiness to distrust of others, too much discipline to rigidity, and too much courage to foolhardiness. When you are telling your story, you can talk about your excesses as well as your deficits.

You work the emotions of your audience by connecting your story to what they hope and fear for their future.

P
A
S
S
I
O
N

The story of your character development provides your audience with a sense of direction and leadership. The story of character is the story of decisions. Your decisions form your character just as your character determines the decisions that you make. Both the decisions you made and those you failed to make are important to your story.

What Are the Skills?

As a spokesperson, you must be the proponent of some new knowledge, ideas, system, or ability. Your function is connecting what you know about an audience's needs, the changes they face, and the lessons of your life story to these skills.

These skills cannot be innate, inborn abilities or skills that require a very specific background. They must be skills anyone can learn. For example, if you are a professional athlete, you cannot talk about your inborn abilities or the technique of your sport to a general audience, but you can talk about what your sport has taught you about teamwork, practice, self-discipline, and other general abilities we all need to develop.

Don't worry if you haven't yet identified the special skills

Your story outlines the development of your character to illustrate how your audience can develop its character.

or knowledge you want to promote. We are going to spend the whole next chapter discussing how you target and package your special expertise. What is important is that these skills relate directly to your real-life experiences. You have to have seen how they work from your personal experience.

When you talk to an audience, you don't have to actually teach them a new skill or ability during the course of your initial talk. As a spokesperson, your job, at least initially, is to get your audience excited about the value of a new skill. This means you have to focus on the benefits of mastering that skill rather than on the details of learning the new skill. A basic presentation is not long enough for anything else.

The most important rule concerning the skills that you champion to an audience is that those abilities must be in tune with your core mission and a need the audience feels.

The "Why" of Our Goals

Finally, you are the spokesperson for your goals and mission. Your mission is your motivation for speaking. It is the true core of your passion. It explains why you are championing a certain set of skills or knowledge or organization or product. Your mission consists of the values and personal philosophy that drive you to get up and speak before an audience.

Cavett Robert, founder of the National Speakers Association said it best. He said, "They don't care how much you know until they know how much you care."

Everyone has a mission whether they realize it or not. Everyone has goals. You have a goal in speaking. Everyone in your audience has a goal in attending. You must connect your mission with their mission. This process starts with understanding your audience's needs, the common ground that brings them together. It ends with a discussion of your mission.

You need to be passionate about the topic you are a spokesperson for if you expect your audience to care as well.

You need a specific objective goal when you speak, a topic we will address in detail later. However, all specific goals start with a longer-term, more general, subjective mission. This mission must be something with which your audience can identify. There are many types of missions but they can all be boiled down to four levels of motivation: economic motivation, professional motivation, emotional motivation, and philosophical motivation.

The most basic of all goals is meeting your immediate economic needs. Over the long term, your goal becomes to build up your professional credibility and relationships. Thinking even longer term, you begin to focus on your emotional relationships with other people. Finally, those who have the longest-term goals focus on basic truths and timeless values.

An audience will understand when your goals are simply economic, but the most persuasive missions are based on long-term values. You must express your values in terms your audience can relate to. Your mission should join your interests with their success in some fundamental way and focus you on helping them meet their needs.

Explaining your mission completes the picture for your audience. It tells them why you are talking to them and why you are passionate about your topic. Your audience only knows your mission if you tell them.

------- 33 -------

P
A
S
S
I
O
N

Similarities and Differences

You need to meet economic goals to continue speaking, but philosophical goals are more persuasive to others.

Common ground, changing times, character, skills, and goals define your relationship with the audience. If you address all five of these areas, your presentation will connect you with the audience. In each of these areas, you must recognize what you share with your audience and how you can offer them a different perspective. Your presentation is defined by your similarity to your audience and your differences from them.

Audiences connect with you because of your similarities to them. These similarities come from what you share with them. You connect with your audience when you establish the following links:

1. You find common ground with their needs.

2. You understand how they feel about the changes they face.

3. Your character is similar to theirs.

4. The knowledge you offer can help them.

5. Your beliefs and goals are similar to their own.

To establish rapport with an audience, you need to identify these connection points. These shared experiences are the basis for presenting your topic and winning your audience.

However, you must do more than just echo your audience's feelings. You must excite them about a new potential future. You do this by highlighting the difference between you and your audience. Audiences want to hear:

1. A new viewpoint on the common ground they share.

2. A different take about the changing times.

3. How they can change their character.

4. About new skills and ideas they can use.

5. About why their success matters to you.

These differences make you valuable to your audience. They make you interesting and believable. These differences give you a unique perspective on their situations. This unique perspective can give them new insight on solving their problems or achieving their goals.

Similarities connect you with your audience. Differences point out new paths you can help them explore.

Notice how everything works for you as a spokesperson. Where you are just like your audience, you connect with them. Where you are different from your audience, you have the basis for educating, entertaining, and convincing your audience you are authentic. The general rule is that you make the connection first, then move the relationship forward by highlighting your differences.

As a spokesperson, you don't have to worry about whether or not you are better or worse than your audience. You only have to understand how your position is both the same as and different from theirs. With each new audience, you will share similarities. With each new audience, you will have differences. You only need to know how to leverage these similarities and differences correctly to get the most emotional mileage out of your presentation.

You and Your Audience

Now you can use these five key connection points to create a template for constructing your story for a given audience. You can create a general template for a general audience now, but you must repeat this exercise every time you speak, using your pre-presentation interview, which we cover in more detail in

Chapter 7. This basic template can be used for speaking on a

Initially, you compare yourself to theoretical audiences. Each real audience offers an opportunity to test your ideas.

variety of topics because it is based on your life experiences, not on any specific expertise or product you are promoting.

You create this template in three steps. First you answer a series of questions comparing and contrasting your experience with those of a generic audience. Then you use your answers to prioritize three lists: your similarities, your differences, and your life lessons. Finally, you create an outline of your life story that you can plug into your presentation.

Fifteen Questions

For each of the five connection points, you ask three questions. The first identifies similarities with audiences. The next identifies differences. The last identifies your life's lessons. Give as many answers to each question as you can. It is perfectly OK if you ask friends and relatives to help you come up with ideas.

1. Common ground: What experiences do you share with most audiences? What experiences set you apart from most audiences? Which of your experiences might others benefit from?

2. Changing times: What well-known trends or changes in society concern you? What changes and trends do you see that others miss? What opportunities do you see in these changes that others might miss?

3. Points of character: What character flaws do you have? What strengths do you have? What character flaws have you overcome?

4. The skills you offer: What skills, hobbies, training, and

knowledge do you have that are very common? What skills, hobbies, training, and knowledge do you have that others might find unusual or interesting? What are the benefits to others of mastering your more unusual skills?

> Speaking is
> an inexpen-
> sive form of
> therapy that
> turns all your
> mistakes into
> life lessons.

5. Your mission: What goals do you share with most audiences? What goals make you unique and interesting? What about your personal philosophy might benefit others?

Make Three Lists

Out of these questions, you end up with three lists of answers. The first is your "connections" list. It identifies five different categories of similarities you have in common with your audience. The next is your "differences" list. It identifies five different categories of different perspectives you can give your audience. The last is your "life lessons" list. It identifies five different categories of what you have learned from your experiences.

Since you can have hundreds of answers and examples from these fifteen questions, you want to prioritize each set of answers. Given all you've learned about connecting to an audience, see if you can identify the most interesting and valuable answer to each of these fifteen questions.

Your Life Story Thus Far

Finally, create sample outlines that tell your life story. Theoretically, all you need is to pick your most interesting where, when, who, what, and why from your lists. The order and number of examples don't matter as long as you get at least one

P
A
S
S
I
O
N

where, when, who, what, and why into your story. You can and should create dozens of different life stories just by playing with your answers and rearranging them in different ways.

Though selecting one area from each of these five topics seems too easy, it automatically creates interesting stories.

For example, you can start with a unique interest, then to a trend everyone sees, then to a character flaw, then move to a skill you mastered, and end with how it shaped your personal goals.

Using this example, let me create one version of my life story. My father died in my arms when I was in my teens. The trend this brings to mind is the way families have changed since the 1960s, when my father died. This leads to my character flaw of oversensitivity, which led me into a first marriage that failed. The skill I mastered was how to continually work on my personal relationships which led to my ideal second marriage. This led to my personal philosophy that all relationships are dynamic and have to be continually developed or they will fail.

Now, this isn't a story that I have ever used, but you can see how well it would fit certain audiences and certain topics. If I wanted to become a spokesperson for a product involving relationships, a book on relationship strategy comes to mind: it tells what I know and why others might want to listen.

More to the point, this story is interesting—not because my life is so interesting, but because it has all the ingredients in our formula. It connects with my audience. It offers an unusual perspective. It provides something the audience can gain from listening to me. Most importantly, it has emotions chords that I can play upon.

This last point is critical. The title of this chapter is "Passion." Your life story sets you up as a spokesperson for your topic. It identifies the right audiences for your presentations. But mostly, your story must explain why you care and why your audience should care as well.

> Your life story can be interesting to your audiences if you take the time to make it interesting.

P
A
S
S
I
O
N

A Few Final Thoughts on Passion

I don't know your life story, but if you use the techniques in this chapter, you can create life stories that will qualify you to become a passionate spokesperson on a number of topics.

You have as much to offer as I did when I started. Your everyday failures, your unique experiences, and what you have learned are your most valuable assets as a spokesperson. It is a shorter distance than you can imagine between your experiences and becoming interesting and influential.

When you start speaking, you will naturally develop more and more interesting perspectives on your life. You will also get more experiences to add to your lists because you will move up in the world. Successful speakers continually answer these questions in more interesting ways.

Your life experiences explain your passion. An important part of that passion is why you care about your audience. As we started this chapter explaining, your success is more dependent on your audience's passions than on your own. You must explain to your audience why you care so very much. Your life story must reinforce your personal philosophy.

—CHAPTER 3—
EXPERTISE
THAT IS INTERESTING

Your Credibility Strategy:
From Average to Expert

An excellent speaker named Natalie had an interesting idea about becoming a "generic" spokesperson. Though she worked in the health industry, she wondered if she could use all the great opportunities open to speakers to become a "hired gun," promoting a variety of businesses. She had heard me talk on strategy and knew I was researching this book on speaking, so she asked me what I thought.

I instantly saw the appeal of the idea, but I had to tell her that it wouldn't work. A hired spokesperson is just another salesperson. No audience gets excited listening to salespeople. Audiences listen to experts.

There are no generic experts. Becoming an expert can be easy, but you cannot become an expert in everything, nor can you make money throwing away your expertise. You make money by developing unique expertise that leads directly to having interesting topics about which you can talk.

The Expertise That Matters

Part of the power of speaking is that it establishes you as an expert. By speaking, you become credible and recognized. Only by speaking can you develop the most valuable form of expertise, the connection of a specific area of knowledge to the broad spectrum of needs. This type of expertise makes more money than any regular skill—a lot more. The only reason that more people don't develop this expertise is because they don't know how easy it is.

Only by speaking can you connect a specialized area of interest to the broad spectrum of people's needs.

Becoming a valuable expert as a speaker is easier than you can imagine. You don't have to study or work for years or even months. You don't have to be a genius. It's better if you aren't. Audiences need experts who talk like regular people.

In the last chapter, you discovered the different ways your life story can distinguish you from your audience. You now need to connect your story to an area of expertise. This expertise becomes the basis for your topic or topics as a speaker.

Your authority doesn't come from knowing your topic so well that no one else can understand you when you talk. It comes from explaining an area of knowledge so well that your average audience member can see the value in it. There has been and always will be a shortage of these practical experts in every field of knowledge. You can start becoming that expert today.

Your opportunity for developing expertise often starts at work. You can be immediately rewarded if you are perceived as an expert by your fellow workers. Developing this expertise is easy. You only need to focus on a topic that your coworkers are interested in but do not have time to study themselves. If you study this topic and start talking about it, you establish yourself as the "in-house" expert. This makes you instantly more valuable at your workplace.

In the late seventies, I was selling consumer products for Bic Pen. At the time, computer inventory systems began to change how our products were ordered. Since I was comfortable with computers, I began studying how the use of computers affected ordering and made a presentation to several people in my organization.

Most people can instantly start making more money by becoming recognized as an expert in their workplace.

After that presentation, I became the "go-to" guy for many in my part of the company with computer questions. This forced me to learn more about computers. The eventual result was that within a few years, I got into the computer industry. I kept speaking and this led to starting my own software company and my eventual financial independence.

Because I stood up to speak, I positioned myself as the expert. Because I continued to speak, I became recognized as an expert on computers and the authority on my particular area of software—so much so that my articles were published in the trade journals and one of my books became a college textbook.

Many people in the computer industry and even my own company knew much more about the technology than I did. My expertise was more valuable because I connected that technology to the concerns of ordinary people.

The Typical Topics of Speakers

A speakers bureau can list up to 30,000 professional speakers. Every one of those people considers himself or herself an expert in some topic. However, most of them work in a very narrow range of what I call the "typical topics."

Typical topics include accounting, bookkeeping, borrowing, conflict resolution, customer service, design, diversity, entrepreneurship, ethics, feedback, goal setting, health/wellness, investing, job markets, leadership, management, motivation, negotiating, nonverbal signals, objectives, planning, presentation, priorities, problem solving, productivity, quality, question asking, relationships, sales, self-esteem, strategy, substance abuse, teams, technology, telephone use, and writing. This list doesn't include every typical topic. Its purpose is to give you a clear idea of what they are so you can recognize one when you see it.

Too many speakers competing for speaking fees make the mistake of choosing the most generic topics.

These topics exist for an important reason. They address very common problems. People are always looking for advice and insights in these areas. This makes these topics safe for event planners. However, like the safe chicken meals that are regularly served at meetings, people get tired of them.

Most professional speakers speak on more or less the same topics in more or less the same way. Most compete with many other speakers very directly. A basic rule of strategy says that you cannot find success by following the crowd. If you want to offer something more interesting and give yourself a better chance of being heard, you have to break away from the crowd.

More Interesting Topics

Fascinating areas of expertise are not hard to discover but

they are in short supply because everyone plays it safe. There is a simple formula for creating an interesting topic. It comes from Sun Tzu's *The Art of War*. Sun Tzu wrote that you use the direct approach to engage the enemy but you use surprise to win. In other words, you can manufacture valuable expertise—and great topics—by combining what is expected with what is unexpected.

Combining new and old creates interesting topics. People relate to the old part and are intrigued with the new part.

If you don't know what your area of expertise should be, you can use this approach to create a new one. The different versions of your life story point you in the right direction. From there, you only need to combine a common interest with one of your unique ones.

1. Pick one area from the list of typical topics.

2. Pick another area from your own more unusual personal interests. It can be anything from astrophysics to zithers.

3. Combine to apply to the lives of regular people.

Most speakers get this recipe exactly wrong. If they combine topics, they mix two or even three of the common topics and forget about adding something new. The result is a plethora of "blah-blah" topics such as priority negotiating, self-esteem planning, or—wait, this one is almost interesting—nonverbal phone use.

Interesting topics require a dash of the unusual, a pinch of the unknown, or a splash of odd. They should sound different. For, example, do you want to hear someone talk about problem-solving management (yawn!) or about what you can learn from how sharks solve survival problems in the ocean?

I personally discovered the power of the unusual when I started talking about Sun Tzu's *The Art of War*. Before that I was talking about typical topics such as database design and planning for change. It wasn't until I added the 2,500-year-old secrets of Sun Tzu into the mix that things started getting really interesting to my audiences.

You find new angles from life experience to address the recurring problems addressed by professional speakers. Sometimes it is just a new perspective on an old challenge. For example, when my daughter Amanda was designing web sites, she told me about a discipline called "experience design," which looked at web sites from the perspective of how users experienced them. Couldn't a few rules from this new discipline improve just about any customer interaction that people plan?

As a spokesperson, authentic passion for your topic is more important than any other credentials you can have.

One advantage of this approach is its freshness, but another is that it leverages your personal passion. This passion makes the topic more interesting because it connects it to your life story. When you talk about areas of expertise that are part of your life, the audience knows it and feels it. This gives you authenticity.

Authenticity and Credibility

In most cases, your credibility as an authority comes simply from speaking on your topic. This is true for virtually all professional speakers who talk about those typical topics. No colleges or universities are giving degrees in priority negotiating. No universities are offering courses in self-esteem planning.

Despite this almost complete lack of credentials in the world of speaking, a great deal of money is being made. This nonac-credited training marketplace accounts for forty billion dollars in sales per year. Only a small fraction of this is paid as tradi-tional speaking fee, where almost all the competition is, but speaking, in one form or another, generates all these sales.

After a steady diet of tradi-tional speak-ing fare, most audiences are hungry for new, interesting observations.

For a unique and interesting twist on a typi-cal topic, your credibility is never a matter of education or professional training. Your cred-ibility always comes from your life story, your experiences, and your interests. For example, if you had a close encounter with a shark, you might naturally become interested in sharks. This puts you in the position of making unique observations. For example, how do the ways sharks solve problems compare with the ways most people solve problems? You do not need a degree in marine biology to become the leading expert in this unique area of expertise.

Why aren't most professional speakers better at specializing their expertise? Because they are trying to make a living on speaking fees. This means that they think they need to cast as wide a net as possible. Books targeting professional speakers advise them to broaden their expertise as much as possible so that they can get hired to speak on any topic to any audience.

This approach is bad strategy, especially if you want to be successful at making money rather than just professional speaking. In the science of strategy, we call this a "spread-out" position, which is the most difficult position to defend. In general, most really successful people narrow their focus so that they can get better and better at what they do.

To become a valuable expert you need to focus. You need to

be unique. You need the authenticity that comes from your life story, but a small amount of experience can connect you to a broad range of human interests. You can pick any topic whose principles can help people in their everyday lives.

Fleshing Out Your Expertise

Though your life story positions you to talk on a certain topic, you will almost certainly need to flesh out your knowledge. The process of collecting in-depth information in any narrow area of expertise is simpler than you imagine.

Developing a depth of knowledge in one or two areas that most people do not have is simply a matter of focus.

1. Start with one typical topic and one unusual interest.
2. Obtain four or more books on each area, both the latest works and those that have stood the test of time.
3. Read those books over several weeks while taking detailed notes.

After reading four books and taking notes on any topic, you will have plenty of information to simplify the topic for the average person. Your notes will have captured a wealth of detailed information. You will also have learned what other experts agree upon and what they do not.

Of course, if you want, you can get more training in your area of expertise. You can take academic courses, go through the library, attend adult classes, join associations, read magazines and newspapers, attend seminars and lectures and so on.

However, there are many reasons not to get caught up in

study. Too often, it serves as an excuse for not getting out and speaking. The time study requires is better used speaking on your topic. Starting with too much information makes it harder to simplify the knowledge for average people. It often also makes you less certain of your observations. You could also start to lose interest.

Successful spokespeople don't know more. They just organize what they know in more interesting ways.

Another source of information on your topic is the Internet. The web, however, is less an information resource than a competitive and market research tool. You should go on the web and see what is out there, if only to get a sense of who is active in related areas of expertise. This competitive knowledge is a good basis for further specializing your expertise.

Blending Two Topics

You now have more information about your topic, but it doesn't yet qualify as "expertise." Before you can call yourself an expert, you need to come up with some unique insights. Fortunately, there is an easy way to do this.

1. Use one of the standard approaches to organize the information you have collected.

2. Start by organizing your typical topic and unusual interests separately.

3. Use your unusual interest to select which concepts you will embrace from the typical topic.

4. Reorganize your material, mixing both topics together where they can be connected.

5. Reorganize again to highlight the insights you gain from mixing your two topics together.

Information isn't knowledge until it is organized. Knowledge doesn't make you an expert until you can solve people's problems. Speakers don't need to know more than technical experts. They just need to be better organized.

You must reorganize what you've learned to make it simpler, more relevant, and more interesting to your audience. This is why combining your unusual interest with a typical topic is important. A typical topic represents the common problems and needs. Your unusual interest represents something new and interesting. By putting them together, you are able to offer a unique perspective on common problems.

Speaking is a valuable service because it forces you to organize knowledge so others can understand it more easily.

Each topic suggests its own order. Start with what is easy. Some information is easily organized by chronological order or by geographical location. You can use the order of increasing difficulty or list the most common situations first. You can use the deductive order: a generalization that is supported by details. Or you can use the inductive order: specific examples that lead to a general idea. The organization scheme you choose should help in presenting your perspective to your audience.

Your main job is to decide what is important to the average audience member and what is not. Technicians are interested in details. You should be interested in what your audience finds useful. While undertaking this task, you start creating your own point of view. This requires deciding what is important and what you believe is true.

First focus on what is interesting. Any information that you can connect to your personal story is interesting. Any information that connects the typical topic to your unusual interest is also interesting. Information that just echoes what people have heard before is less interesting and should be used only as connective material to link one idea to another.

The disagreement of experts is also interesting. Some of the

Nothing makes an audience happier than hearing a speaker explain why other experts get it wrong.

material you've collected will offer conflicting views. You shouldn't brush such disagreements aside. You want to use them in your presentation. If you can explain why some authorities are wrong, you automatically become an expert on experts.

Which side you take is less important than your willingness to take a stand. The more controversial your stand, the better it is for your audience. People want to hear ideas that are different from conventional wisdom. Nothing makes an audience happier than hearing you declare other experts wrong.

Making judgments about what is true and why is easier than it sounds. The answer lies in the intersection of the typical topic and your unusual interest. You pick the point of view that fits best for your blended topic as a whole.

You have already seen an example of this. At least one book on speaking advises speakers to develop broad, general topics, while others suggest more focused topics. For my personal point of view, the principles of strategy served as my tiebreaker.

Mixing the two areas of knowledge is the fun part. Usually, the typical boring topics have the better-developed frameworks for organization. You can use that framework and mix the quirky, unusual information from your special interest to illustrate and illuminate that organization. Any two topics can be mixed.

Even more exciting, you can occasionally use your unusual interest to reorganize how a typical topic can be taught. For example, you can explain the recent evolution of the use of statistics in baseball and apply those lessons to good management practices.

In a few cases, your unusual interest will allow you to completely reinvent a typical, overworked topic into something new and exciting. This certainly proved true in my use of Sun Tzu's *The Art of War* in redefining the discussion business strategy. My experience with *The Art of War* demonstrates what can happen when you explore your unusual interest in a new context. However, you may find that strategy can offer even more, helping you develop you own special form of expertise.

> *Simply by combining two ideas together for the first time, you can create a powerful recipe for success.*

Adding Strategy to Expertise

In any discussion of expertise, I would be remiss if I didn't introduce you to the advantages of using the science of strategy. The science of strategy applies the well-defined rules of military combat to other competitive arenas. If your topic involves meeting challenges, strategy provides a wealth of useful ideas.

The science of strategy provides a framework for organization. It relates everything to the few ingredients that build competitive positions. For example, the five connection points for your life story discussed in the previous chapter—common ground, the changing times, character, skills, and goals—come straight from the first pages of Sun Tzu's definition of a strategy position.

At the Science of Strategy Institute, our trainers apply standard strategic methods to meeting challenges in competitive arenas from romance to parenting to common business challenges. This approach provides audiences with a valuable new perspective from which they can better understand their situation.

You can use the principles of strategy to quickly add depth and perspective to any topic dealing with challenge.

You too may find the rules of strategy useful in sharpening your expertise. The following three steps are all that are required.

1. Learn the techniques of strategy from the Science of Strategy Institute.

2. Organize your ideas to follow the principles for defining and advancing a strategic position.

3. Obtain licensing from the Institute to use our presentation materials for your topic.

I discovered how much these principles could improve presentations more than twenty years ago and that discovery has been yielding valuable results ever since—not only for me but for all our trainers.

This approach also gives you instant credibility. You can organize your material according to an established standard. You also take your place as a licensed member of a community that understands and teaches to that standard. You even get a training license you can hang on your wall.

As a good personal interest should, the strategic method refines your topic to distinguish what you talk about from what other speakers are offering. You can promote your own unique vision from within an umbrella organization that legitimizes you. Strategic science and the strategic method are a powerful addition to the traditional knowledge important to a specific area of expertise.

Refining Your Expertise

With your personal story, a typical topic, a unique interest, a little research, and some reorganizing, you can quickly develop a very strong new perspective for becoming a persuasive spokesperson. However, at this point, your mixture is still raw and unproven. You have to test and refine your recipe against the curiosity and interests of real audiences.

> *Your personal story and research into your topic provide a solid basis for creating presentations that you can test.*

Through the rest of this book, we will introduce you to a number of other well-established formulas for refining your expertise. You will learn how to make products, how to address various venues, how to make a presentation and, most importantly, how you can turn this knowledge into money. But these processes all depend upon you testing your work in front of audiences.

The only way to see what really connects with audiences is by getting in front of them and talking to them. When you get up and talk, especially at first, you are experimenting with your ideas and testing how you have organized them for presentation. You only need to develop them far enough so that you can test them in front of an audience.

As we will explain in great detail in Chapter 5, when you start speaking you begin speaking to the safest possible audiences. To those initial groups, your topic only has to be interesting enough to arouse curiosity. If your topic wins you the opportunity to speak, it puts you in a position to learn more about what audiences want.

Through the feedback system explained in detail in Chapter 7, your audiences themselves will tell you what more they need to know and what additional research you need to do if

There are a number of aspects to refining your expertise discussed in this book, but all of them depend on your speaking.

necessary. Through this process, your expertise grows more and more valuable because you are adapting your material to what your audiences tell you is important.

This process takes time. It also takes a willingness to get out in front of audiences before you are "ready." The point is that you cannot get ready without working with audiences and getting feedback. Your material in the beginning will be the worst it will ever be, but it will also be the best you can have without taking it out for a spin.

This process starts in venues where speaking is only a little more formal than chatting with friends. It could even start by addressing people within your company or community groups who know you. You learn from your early speaking opportunities so that you can move up to more valuable and demanding venues. Presentations are not just opportunities to talk: they are opportunities to listen, learn, and develop your expertise.

Only audiences can tell you what they would like to know. Only a range of audiences can give you perspective into what different kinds of people would like to learn about your topic. Over time, you will get more good ideas from your audiences than they get from you.

Each speaking opportunity builds up your knowledge on how to connect your topic with people's needs. Each engagement builds up your ability to express your ideas more clearly and persuasively. Speaking builds up your confidence and increases your understanding of how to tailor your topic to different people's needs.

You want audiences asking questions that you can't answer. Only when they do can you know what answers to look for. Even without the more formal systems of collecting feedback that we will introduce you to, you cannot help but learn more about your topic, especially on how valuable it is to people, if you have the courage to stand up and talk about it.

> *Speaking is more than an opportunity to be heard. It is an opportunity to listen and learn people's interests.*

This is what we mean when we say that money-making expertise comes solely from speaking. There are many types of experts. The type of expert that you become by studying a topic for your own curiosity alone, without getting feedback from others, is not valuable to others. Only by talking to others do you learn what they find valuable.

Make It Valuable

Remember, it is never about how great your knowledge is; it is about how your knowledge can make others great. Making money is important because it places a quantifiable number on the value that you produce. To keep yourself focused on producing value, follow these steps:

1. After going through the exercises in this book, prepare a presentation and speak at a beginner's-level event.

2. Collect audience feedback to identify what you can improve.

3. Make improvements and speak at the same level of event again.

4. Collect feedback again and see if more improvements are still needed.

5. When you are confident in your material, move up to the next level of event, and speak again.

Speaking gives you practice, hones your knowledge, creates a track record, and expands your contacts.

6. Move up through the various levels of venues to find the audience that pays the best rewards.

This gradual approach makes failure impossible and setbacks rare. It gives you an opportunity to practice and perfect your presentation. It teaches you speaking skills one step at a time. It creates the track record that gives you more credibility as an expert. It expands your base of contacts, which makes it easier and easier to generate income.

As you go through the process, you will find that your topic can quickly evolve and change. If you take your cue from your audiences, you will direct your learning in ways that you could never have planned. You can only discover these opportunities if you get out to speak. As long as you are out speaking, you are positioned to discover opportunities.

This process builds your credibility as an expert. By speaking, you naturally acquire testimonials and references. Everyone who enjoys and learns from your presentation is equally valuable. For a speaker, testimonials from average people are more valuable than credentials from a university.

The Perception of Expertise

Audiences make their decisions based solely upon their perceptions of you as a speaker. At first, audiences may assume that you know more than you do. Perception is reality, and it also creates reality. You will discover that, over time, what you learn and know conforms to your audiences' expectations of what you should know. In the end, you come to know exactly what your audiences expect you to know.

You change people's perceptions of you by standing up and speaking. This transformation can be difficult when people think they already know you. If you have been working with the same people for ten years, it will be very difficult to change your coworkers' impression of you. When you talk to those who are just getting to know you, you can quickly and easily shape their perception of your expertise.

Speaking brings you into contact with people who do not know you and this allows you to easily redefine who you are.

You always have to be concerned with the impression you make on people. Learning to make a good impression as a speaker carries over to every other aspect of your life.

You want to make a good first impression, but you also want to exceed people's expectations. For example, when you join a new company, you want opportunities to speak on topics on which you are knowledgeable, but you need to be humble about what you know. You want to develop your status as an expert gradually, without making claims that create expectations that you cannot satisfy.

It is much safer to downplay the depth of your expertise at first. Instead, you focus on the interesting insights and entertaining aspects of your topic. If you accept the idea that you are going to advance your position step by step, you never have to exaggerate your abilities. You want to appear less prepared than you are. You never emphasize or apologize for your lack of experience, but you want to pleasantly surprise audiences.

This is why your life story should start with your frailties and mistakes. We have all embarrassed ourselves in the past. This connects you to your audience. Authentic experts don't build themselves up. They have a clear sense of how much more they have to learn. Only fakers have to puff themselves up, but if they do, they are setting themselves up for a fall.

Be humble: true experts are those who appreciate how much they still have to learn better than anyone else.

Present your expertise as fresh, different, and unique rather than highly polished and proven. This novelty alone attracts an audience. Then, if you follow through using the techniques in this book, you cannot help but impress those who hear you.

You will discover from your audiences whether or not your topic is valuable or not. If it is, it will inevitably lead you to money-making opportunities. If it doesn't make money, you improve it until it does. People will pay for expertise.

When I began to establish myself as an expert on computers at Bic Pen, I had no idea how expertise would pay. It began paying dividends almost immediately. Within a year, I became the salesperson of the year based on my newfound understanding of how computers were changing the way that buyers ordered products. Of course, I could never have guessed that the ultimate payoff for learning about computers would be starting my own software company.

A Few Final Thoughts on Expertise

In the last two chapters, you have learned how to put your life experiences and interests into the context of an audience's needs. These methods enable you to identify potential topics and areas in which you can develop expertise. By speaking, you will learn the value of this expertise or how it leads to value. By listening to your audiences, you will refine this expertise so that it becomes more and more valuable. And as you develop your expertise by speaking, you will build your knowledge and credibility.

Advancing your expertise is like climbing a ladder. That ladder must be placed solidly on your current position. You start with your experience and interests. You base your expertise on a life story that is interesting and appealing.

As you read the next several chapters, you discover plenty of ways to polish your expertise before speaking.

You take one step up the ladder by doing some very focused research to connect your interests to what people are looking for from speakers. By working to bring something different to the typical problems that speakers address, you develop a new perspective that can interest and entertain audiences, at least as a novelty.

As you move through the other steps in this book, you will test your ideas against the demands made on spokespeople. In the next chapter, you will see if your expertise makes sense as a product. In the chapter after that, you will see how well it fits into speaking opportunities available. Then you will see how well it works in a typical presentation. Each step will reshape your ideas about what your expertise should be.

If you speak on your topic regularly, you cannot help but develop the type of expertise that is valuable to people. The more valuable your expertise, the more money you must make.

CHAPTER 4

ASSETS
TO PROMOTE

Your Sales Strategy:
From Hours to Products

When you stand up to talk, it is understood that you have a point to make. What is less well understood is that if you are going to continue to invest time in speaking, you need a return on the efforts you invest. Becoming a spokesperson consumes time and resources. You cannot continue to speak unless you are rewarded by the speaking in some tangible way. You certainly cannot make money from speaking unless you make the process pay.

As a spokesperson, you work to persuade others. What is it that you want to persuade them to do? How will their decision help you? As an expert, you are selling in an extremely subtle way, but you are still selling. The term "spokesperson" suggests that there is a cause or product you are championing. This strategy only works if you have a clear general goal you are working toward and specific rewards you want to win along the way.

You want to make it easy for your audiences to act as a result of your presentation. That action must benefit you.

In this chapter, you will see how you can offer your expertise in a broad range of assets. We call these assets "products"
because they are produced from your expertise. After you speak,
you always want your audience to want more of you. This
means that you must package your knowledge so that they can
get more of you easily.

What is the point of speaking, really? You aren't going
to change your audience members' minds or habits in a few
minutes. People only remember 10 percent of what they hear.
It takes two weeks to create a new habit. No
skill worth teaching is taught in the course of a
single speech.

Audiences need products to help them remember what they heard and to turn their new knowledge into valuable habits.

You are going to get their interest with
your newly developed topic or expertise. The
question is: What do you think you can do
with that interest? How can you turn it to your
advantage? Your audiences will tell you what
they want, but how do you want to channel
their interest?

The most a speech can do is convince the audience of the
value of getting more involved with your topic, you, or your
organization. If you are really going to improve the lives of
the members of your audience, you need to tell them how to
take the next step. You are doing your audiences a disservice if
you get them excited about your ideas but don't give them any
direction about what they need to do next.

You must know what decision you want your audience to
make. This is a service that you provide. Even if you want them
to buy someone else's books to learn more about your topic,
you need to give them direction. You develop your product

around your presentation while simultaneously developing your presentation around your product.

You can be a spokesperson for virtually any type of asset. You can speak to convince people to hire you, to promote you, to work with your organization, or simply to buy one product or another. This product can change from audience to audience. When you speak within your company, you are selling one type of personal asset. When you speak about your company, you are selling another. A big part of deciding where and when to talk and what to say comes from knowing what you are promoting and to whom.

Design your assets around your speaking. Design your speaking around your assets.

Product Strategy

You develop your assets in the same way you develop your expertise, one easy step at a time, relying on feedback from your audiences. You start with the easiest products to acquire and sell. You then work up to more and more sophisticated and profitable products.

Before we get to the specifics of identifying, acquiring, and developing these assets, you should understand one more important point: what you appear to be promoting during your presentation isn't necessarily the asset you are really promoting over the long term.

As a spokesperson, you often work like a magician. You use misdirection to control your audience's experience. You direct your audience's attention in one direction, toward your expertise, as a way of avoiding the natural reflex of sales resistance.

The necessity for this deception is rooted in human psychology. The science of strategy teaches that when you push people, they naturally push back. The most successful speakers and spokespeople never use a "hard sell." You make money because you are enthusiastic about the value of an idea, not the money-making consequences of that value.

However, you cannot and need not deny the fact that you are offering something of value to your audience. The members of your audience want to know why you are speaking. They want to understand your mission. In other words, they already know you are promoting something. They are curious about what it might be.

> *Speaking is part of a funnel deepening customer relationships. Your products continue those relationships.*

Early in your presentation, you want to put your audience at ease. You can tell them directly what your mission is, but you are more subtle about telling them that you want them to act. You always put your product in terms of the benefit you want to produce for them not the benefit you receive in return.

The best product to sell is a long-term relationship with your audience. You must be sincere about that relationship.

For example, I am writing this book because I sincerely believe that you can become more successful and make more money if you become a spokesperson and an expert. This book offers you a lot of great ideas you can use, but the Science of Strategy Institute offers a lot more. We not only make it easy for you to use the spokesperson strategy, but the more successful you are, the more you need our other training in strategy.

As you develop your own assets over time, you will see how your initial offering is simply the first step in this relationship with your audience. Long-term relationships are the key to your financial success. Selling people one product one time is never profitable. The only successful businesses are those that bring customers back again and again for more. Repeat business is the key to making money.

One reason the most successful speakers do not use a hard sell is because they want to get invited back to speak again and again to the same events. You want your presentation to one group to lead to references to other, similar groups. In other words, you develop your position as a spokesperson by developing relationships.

When you position yourself as a spokesperson and an expert, you are telling your audience you have more to offer.

The most successful spokespeople think of their presentations as part of a much larger funnel. Their presentations are the wide mouth of this funnel. The goal at first is to get people interested. Then the assets you offer make it easy for people to move down in this funnel, developing a closer and closer relationship with you and your organization.

Your assets and products are designed to keep customers happily involved. They form a chain or a pipeline. Each product leads customers to the next product. The pipeline keeps them in the funnel. Each product is part of the continuing relationship you begin by speaking. You continually bring new customers into the funnel by continuing to speak. Meanwhile, your product pipeline continues to give them good reasons to continue and deepen that relationship.

The Best Products to Sell

The best product is a long-term relationship, but what does that mean when you are just starting? There are many traditional products that regular speakers sell: training materials, books, tapes, and more extensive training. These products are important for a variety of reasons, which we will discuss later, but they are also the least interesting products for a true spokesperson and expert. They are often also the least profitable.

For a spokesperson-in-training, these products take time and effort to develop, especially if you are just iden-tifying your area of expertise and testing it with audiences. You will eventually want to develop these products because they play an important part in the customer funnel and product pipeline, but you don't have to worry about them when you are first starting.

Your first and most important product is your-self. You must always leave the audience wanting more of you.

When you are just beginning to speak, you should concentrate on selling three more basic and important assets: 1) yourself, 2) your organi-zation, and 3) someone else's products.

You are always the core product. You are always selling the audi-ence on yourself. You can speak to position yourself as a candidate for promotion within your company. You can speak to sell yourself as a resource for other companies, that is, to get hired either as an employee or a consultant. You can speak to qualify yourself as a business partner.

Whenever you speak, your goal is to excite your audience about your viewpoint. At the end of your presentation, they should see the value in getting more. If you have nothing else, you can sell them your time. Your time is the least profitable product because it is the most costly. It cannot be duplicated so there is only so much of it. Selling yourself by the hour is the least profitable way to sell your time. However, you have to start from where you are. When you start speaking, the goal is often to win you more money for your time than you can get any other way.

All other products are proxies for your time. The assets we discuss in this chapter are really ways of packaging pieces of yourself for mass consumption. No matter what other products you offer, you must never forget that you are always your most important product.

Good speeches are never sales presentations, but mastering speaking results is the most powerful form of selling.

You must sell people on your organization. In my experience, the organization is the fastest, easiest, and most profitable product to start selling. Whether you own your company or work as an employee, you can sell your company's products and services. If you are promoting a cause, you can raise funds for your organization.

I started speaking doing training inside the companies for which I worked. Then, when I started working for a personal computer company, I began giving seminars at our offices, first for small businesses and then for corporations. I didn't start speaking at independent events until I started my software company. When we were first starting, all we had to sell was our consulting expertise. I began speaking at local Rotaries and chambers of commerce about the new computer technology. As our company grew, I began to speak at computer and other industry events.

You can also be a passionate advocate for the products of others. Think about the people who distribute Mary Kay Cosmetics or Tupperware or any of the dozens of other products that are sold through marketing networks. Most of these people are doing exactly what other spokespeople do. They are organizing their own seminars, developing their own presentations. The most successful of these individuals are often using the methods of successful speakers that we describe in this book.

Even the most successful professional speakers often promote the products of others through their seminars. Initially, Tony Robbins promoted NLP training given by others. He formed a partnership with those more experienced in the field. Dozens of other speakers regularly promote others' products. We all have products that we have bought and loved. Why not make money promoting something you are already passionate about?

Especially for beginning speakers, there are three advantages in selling other people's products: 1) it gives you something to sell immediately, 2) you can be passionate about these products without seeming egotistical, and 3) you can borrow credibility from products that are better known and more proven than you are.

When the time comes to speak up, you have to know what to say and how to say it. You can easily learn what to do.

For example, if you are licensed as a trainer with the Science of Strategy Institute, you not only get presentations to use, you instantly have products—books, audios, and on-line training—to sell. We encourage all our trainers to develop their own products, but until then, you get credibility from our work, and you can start generating income.

You need products to sell. You can sell yourself, your company's products, and other people's products from day one. However, after you get a little bit of practice in front of audiences, you can start developing traditional speakers' products. If you are speaking, you will get many opportunities to sell them. More importantly, people expect you to have these products. You disappoint them if you don't. Having them gives you credibility, establishing you as true expert who has much more to offer.

The "Start Small" Pipeline

Since the goal of the process is to get as many people into the funnel as possible, many product pipelines start with inexpensive products and lead gradually to more expensive ones. For example, a common pipeline for traditional speakers who promote more training in their topic might look like this:

When you start with small products, you bring as many customers into the funnel as painlessly as possible.

1. A report or newsletter for $0-$10.

2. A book for $20-$40.

3. A video or audio collection for $100-200.

4. A half-day or full-day seminar for $300-$500.

5. A boot camp or workshop for $600-$1,200.

In a "start small" product pipeline, the initial product is often free, but to get it, customers must give the speaker their contact information. As a spokesperson, you would then use this contact information to develop a relationship with your former audience members and turn them into long-term customers.

To use this "start small" approach, you need resources to follow up and work with the people in your customer funnel. Though much of this process can be automated, especially using the Internet, you are wasting your time speaking and collecting contact information from audience members if you don't have products to sell. You also need the time and resources needed to follow up with those contacts.

The "Start Big" Approach

There is an opposite approach to the "start small" method. It is, obviously, starting big. This approach is used by some of the most successful speakers. It has the benefit of being simpler and requiring fewer products and less customer management. However, it requires an extremely polished presentation, a well-developed product, and a form of expertise that has proven valuable.

Using this approach, you sell the audience a very big product at the beginning of the process. After all, if you can make a very strong presentation, you know how to get audiences excited enough to act. They are at their peak of excitement right after hearing you speak. Nothing else you can do in the pipeline is as exciting and as motivating as listening to a good spokesperson, live, in person.

When you start with big products, you get enough income right away from each customer to give them great value.

There are many important technical issues in using a "start big" approach. For example, you must use extremely solid money-back guarantees. We will discuss many of these issues when we discuss how to create influential presentations and the nuts and bolts of making sales.

Only being a spokesperson allows you to get people totally committed to your program, that is, your funnel, by starting big. Using every other form of marketing, you must start small. One reason I promote making money through speaking is that it allows you to stand the traditional customer funnel on its head—or its mouth.

As you get more experienced, you will also discover that products tailored to the specific needs of an industry command more money than generic products. As you focus your expertise on smaller and smaller segments of the market, you develop more and more specialized products that command higher and higher prices. In almost every area, there are competitors selling generic products. There is always a shortage of industry-specific information.

A vertical focus develops more and more specialized products that command higher and higher prices.

Finally, don't worry about developing the perfect product. As Voltaire noted, the perfect is the enemy of the good. You can continually improve, refine, specialize, and adapt the product over time.

This is part of the general process of refining your expertise one step at a time. This is especially important to remember when you are just starting and need to sell any products that you can.

Selling Time

Many people use the spokesperson strategy to enhance the value of their time. When I started my own company, I sold my time and the time of my associates as computer consultants. The reason that we were successful enough to make the transition to a software company was because we were paid very well for our time based upon the credibility I built through my presentations.

A general rule for selling time profitably is to get away from hourly rates. Instead, you create products that package your time into projects. This focuses the discussion on the value of the project, not on what you or your associates are getting for their time.

Speaking and Training Products

There are too many different ways you can sell your expertise as a consultant to cover even briefly in this book. However, we must discuss the most common way speakers sell their time, that is, by speaking and training.

Every presentation is a product because you can charge a fee for it under the right circumstances. Celebrity speakers charge from $20,000 to $75,000 per speech. Well-known speakers charge $10,000 to $20,000. Established speakers like myself charge from $2,000 to $10,000. Upcoming speakers charge from $500 to $2,000.

You always focus customers on the value they are receiving rather than how much you are charging for your time.

Since you are going to be speaking, you need to know the various terms that people in the industry use to refer to different types of speakers and their presentations. A keynoter gives an opening-session address to a general session, setting a theme of the meeting. A general session presentation is given to a whole group that is sometimes divided into breakout sessions. A breakout session, also called a concurrent session, is one of several presentations taking place at the same time, and attendees choose which session they want to attend. General sessions and concurrent sessions are typically an hour to an hour and a half long, with some time subtracted for breaks and to get to different rooms for concurrent sessions.

After-dinner speakers, which include humorists and character portrayers, those who imitate modern or historical figures
usually talk from twenty to forty minutes. Fees can range from
free to several thousand dollars.

There are also hosts, who act as the central figure at an
event, and moderators, who referee for other speakers. Panelists
offer their expertise as part of group discussion on a specific
topic. Facilitators act as moderators in larger group discussions.
Again, fees for these roles can range from free, as is usually the
case with panelists, to several thousand dollars.

There is a huge range of prices in the world of speaking. How much you can charge depends on how suc-cessful you are.

Presentations

Chapter 6 contains a detailed description
of the most persuasive form of presentation,
but you should understand a little about how
easy it is to prepare presentations in general.
All presentations have three components: 1) a
great opening that grabs your audience's attention, 2) an organized series of "slides," each
illustrating a single idea, with three to four subpoints, grouped
in independent "modules" built around a single point, and 3) a
great ending that gets your audience to act.

That is all there is to it. As you gain more experience, you
develop more modules, making a wider variety of points. More
modules allow you to create longer and more valuable presentation products. During the planning stage of a presentation, you
simply select the modules that are appropriate for a given audience in the time you have.

With more experience, you also develop and acquire more
exercises, stories, quotations, evidence, statistics, illustration,

props, jokes, and other ideas that you can use to illustrate the points you make in your modules.

The most important parts of any presentation are its opening and closing. Once again, we will cover these critical elements in detail later, but remember that the purpose of a presentation is to make an impact on your audience so you can get action. A great opening gets attention, outlines the value of your presentation, and positions you as an expert. In your closing, you highlight what you want your audience to remember and give them a strong incentive to "get happily involved."

Training Products

One of the most common products for speakers to offer is additional training. As you speak you naturally develop more and more material. You can then repackage this material into longer training courses.

Like all products, presentations are made of reusable parts so that everything you do builds up your assets.

Trainers typically offer seminars in half-day (2.5–3.5 hours) or full day (5–6 hours) sessions. They might also offer multiday workshops and boot camps. Prices of seminars can range from free—if you are using them to sell other products—to several hundred dollars per person. Prices of workshops can go as high as several thousand dollars per person.

A corporate training class typically has about fifteen participants. Training employees is a huge market. A 1998 survey determined that employers with fifty or more employees spend an average of $504 per year per employee on training. In 1995, there were 216,300 such training seminars. We can only assume that there are many more today.

Many larger corporations have training departments, but these groups usually hire outside companies for training when requested by an executive. In the Fortune 1000, most outside trainers are paid by the day, not by the number of attendees. The corporation provides the people, room, and refreshments. Many trainers charge an extra fee ($50–$100) for attendees over a certain number (20–25) to discourage corporations from stuffing the class.

Training usually combines lectures, group discussion, and team activities. You can include role-playing, games, multimedia, and even crafts. You can have attendees draw pictures, mold clay, and solve puzzles to make your points. The longer the training, the more variety you want to offer. In any training lasting more than half a day, you need to get people out of their seats. A physical child's game like Simple Simon can keep your audience involved and refreshed.

Corporate training is the most profitable but requires the right topic and corporate champions of your expertise.

One easy way to develop training programs, and make money doing it, is to work with other partners. Colleges, junior colleges, and local civic centers often offer a variety of nonaccredited, adult education courses for which they charge students per head and split the fees with you. There are also a number of public seminar companies including CareerTrack/Fred Pryor, National Seminars, and Dun and Bradstreet. Some of these companies hire and train speakers to give their proprietary training programs. There are also urban independent training companies such as the Learning Annex that charge $39–$99 per attendee for various types of programs.

All these companies are great training grounds for learning, developing, and practicing the development of more advanced training products. We will discuss these partnerships in the next chapter.

More advanced speakers can develop weekend "personal growth experiences" at the high end of the training spectrum. You can offer these seminars in exotic locations anywhere in the world. You can charge up to $1,500 per person for these events. They combine a vacation with the educational (and often tax) benefits of a training program. These programs are usually limited to a dozen people.

Written Material

After speaking, the most powerful form of marketing is the written word. Written products are more profitable than speaking or training because they don't consume your limited time. They can also be reused in a variety of forms.

Adult education for colleges and training companies is not well paid but it provides a great foundation of skills.

If you believe in your message and your ideas, you must write them down. Speaking is more emotionally powerful than writing, but listeners only remember 10 percent of what they hear. Skills are best learned through repetition and you can read written materials over and over again. You can continue to access written materials throughout the approximately fourteen-day period it takes to establish a new habit.

Articles

By writing articles, you get free publicity and increase your credibility. They give you material and promote your speaking.

They also force you to organize your thoughts and generate new ideas. You can give them as handouts, sell them as products, and collect them into books.

When I was speaking to promote my software company, I started writing articles for the computer trade magazines. After a year or so of doing that, I had enough material that I was able to collect it in my first book. At that point a light went on, and I started consciously writing articles as the basis for future books.

You start with local or special-topic newsletters. You then move on to local weekly newspapers. Then you move to trade association newsletters, regional magazines, and trade magazines. Anyone can write at this level. A lucky few can move up to get their material published by national business publications or larger daily newspapers, or even get regular columns.

With writing as with speaking, you start with the easiest places to get articles and work your way up.

To get your articles published, choose a topic that is relevant to the publication and that is based on a topic that is interesting right now. You have to justify why you are the person to write on your topic based on your personal story and experience.

You should research a publication, studying the types of articles it publishes before sending an inquiry about submitting an article. Then send your inquiries to a specific editor's attention. Detail what you are writing about, why their readers would care, and give examples. Tell the editor the length of the article and its delivery date. It is always a good idea to compare what you are doing with other articles that the publication has published. When you write to a publisher, request the specifications for an article and always enclose a self-addressed and stamped envelope to get information back from them.

The best way to write an article is to copy a previous article from the publication to get a general outline. Then, plug in your research and life experiences. Do not use the article to promote your products or services. Use as many specific examples, numbers, names, places, and dates as possible. If your article is rejected, rewrite it slightly and resubmit it again and again to similar publications. Your persistence will pay off.

Newsletters

The next step up from single articles is publishing your own regular newsletters. Newsletters are both a product and, more and more commonly, a marketing device. A few newsletters are still printed and mailed in the traditional way, but the vast majority of newsletters are now electronic. When you start a newsletter, all the articles you have ever written become content for your newsletter.

Research from speaking is reused in articles. Articles are reused in newsletters and reused again in books.

As a product, newsletters are a way to get customers into your product pipeline. In many cases, newsletters are offered for free. They keep your customers updated about what you are doing and remind them of the value you offer. They are especially important for letting customers know about other new products you are offering.

Books

As you develop a growing body of written material on your

area of expertise, most of it can eventually go together into a book. While you can develop a book from scratch, we don't recommend it, at least not for your first book.

You can invite your customers, partners, or other authorities to contribute to a book. However, you should never hire a ghostwriter. You need to do the work yourself if it is to be authentic. Schedule writing on a regular basis. If you are not having the work published somewhere, have others review what you are writing.

Books need to be published, but you can do it yourself. My first half-dozen or so books were published by major publishers, the first three by Bantam Books, but finding a publisher is extremely difficult. While a publisher pays for editing, proofreading, cover design, printing, distribution, and related costs, the disadvantages outweigh the advantages.

> A good-looking and well-designed book gives you instant credibility. A badly designed book doesn't.

Finding a publisher takes too much time because you are competing with fifteen to twenty thousand other authors. Because the publisher pays for printing, you have no control over the product. It takes well over a year or two to get the book finished. In the end, you have to do all the marketing and you only get a small percentage of the sales. You also have to buy your books from your publisher to sell them.

I recommend that all spokespeople self-publish their books. Self-publishing gives you total control over the product. Once it is written, you can get the book printed in a few weeks.

Self-publishing is not easy. First, you do take all the risks. You need to hire, select, and pay your editors, proofreaders, cover designers, and printers. You have to master technical issues regarding design. One bad hire can ruin your work. It will be very difficult for you to get into mainstream bookstore distribution. You will also have to store the books you have printed.

A good initial starting place is "on-demand" publishing, which allows you to print books in small runs as you need them. This costs quite a bit more per book that regular printing, but it lowers your initial printing and storage costs.

At the Science of Strategy Institute, we help our trainers get their first books published. We can provide you with templates for both book and cover design. We can also give you access to our proofreaders and graphic artists if you need them.

Self-publishing makes the most sense given today's technology but it still requires a lot of knowledge.

When your book is finished, you can then print it on demand. If you want to invest in inventory, we can take it to our short-run (up to a thousand copies, paperback only) or full-service printers. If it meets our standards, we can even distribute it to the bookstore market through Clearbridge Publishing, our publishing division.

Audio and Video Products

Audio and video products are the easiest and more profitable products for speakers to sell. Digital recorders and cameras make it easy to record any of your presentations. Computer technology makes editing and duplication fairly easy. You do not want anyone taping your presentations unless you control the masters. Some corporations like to tape presentations for internal distribution or library usage, but you should charge 50 percent more for giving them taping rights. You also want to limit their distribution.

You can also create audio products without even giving a live presentation. You just outline the presentation material and then have someone interview you, asking a series of questions that leads you through your outline.

You can also create audio programs by interviewing other experts and selling the result. A friend of mine, Alex Carrol, an expert in publicity, regularly interviews other experts in marketing and promotion. He offers these interviews initially as free teleseminars but then creates audio products out of them that he sells on his web site.

You can use the Internet to distribute digital content as downloads or offer them to subscribers for on-line access.

While audio and video products can be sold as single discs for twenty to thirty dollars, the most common practice is to bundle them in albums, kits, or collections. You can charge hundreds of dollars for the collection. Most speakers never package their audio or video products for retail sales. Retail packaging is prohibitively expensive. Mostly the audio and video discs are sold in simple plastic cases. The label is printed on the disc alone by an inexpensive inkjet printer.

More and more often, digital content isn't packaged at all. It is downloaded from a web site. The process is easily automated, making it one of the easiest and most profitable products to sell. You can offer free versions of your digital products on audio or video blogs.

Marginal Products

There are dozens of other products you can develop and sell, but beware the law of diminishing returns. Adding more and more products makes the process of maintaining, tracking, and shipping inventory more and more difficult. You can end up tying up a lot of money in inventory while those products sit on the shelf and get outdated.

Among the other more marginal products you can sell are appointment books, calendars, checklists, desktop reference guides, inspirational merchandise, playing cards, quotes on cards, and so on.

A Few Final Thoughts on Assets

The traditional range of speakers' products are important in developing your asset pipeline and customer funnel, and they will generate a constant stream of income from your expertise. They are especially easy to sell via your web site.

You want to advance your position by developing bigger and bigger products, not smaller and smaller ones.

These products serve a purpose but you make much more money as a spokesperson than a pitchman. Ideally, you want to sell bigger concepts and more valuable products, especially as you develop your skill. Look for new and creative ways to profit from what you are passionate about. Look for ways to develop partnerships in which you can use your expertise to leverage the businesses of others.

You must have a product. You must know what your product is. You cannot be successful as a speaker if you do not know how you want your audience to take action.

Chapter 5

Key Steps
Up in Audience

Your Growth Strategy:
From Back Rooms to Boardrooms

Now that you have a story to tell, an expertise, and products, you need an audience. Fortunately, in every city, hundreds of groups have audiences. Every day, there are meetings, conferences, and events. Every year, there are millions of speaking opportunities. Clubs want speakers to address their members. Companies are looking for speakers to teach their employees. Meeting planners need speakers for their events.

My earlier analogy of a ladder most accurately describes the world of speaking. Each level of speaking leads to a higher one. The good news is that you can start harvesting the fruits of your efforts from the lowest steps. Small, local meetings start you painlessly. You use them to develop your skills and references and move up through the speaking hierarchy to where your opportunities are richest.

Even working at the lowest level, you can directly and personally contact thousands of people a year. At the highest levels, tens of thousands can hear you.

The Eight Key Steps

Whenever and wherever you speak, you want to get invited back again and again, year after year. As you move to higher steps in the speaking hierarchy, you may not have the time to work the lower levels, but you may still want to visit them to safely test radically new approaches. Jay Leno still worked small clubs when he was hosting the Tonight Show to try new material. In this chapter, we examine eight key steps in moving up the speaking ladder.

These steps are: 1) unaffiliated clubs, 2) affiliated organizations, 3) local businesses and other organizations, 4) colleges and educational institutions, 5) local conventions and visitors' bureaus, 6) seminar and event promoters, 7) your own public seminars, and 8) the corporate marketplace.

You also need to know about a few other entities in the speakers' universe: speakers showcases, speakers bureaus, and agents.

Unaffiliated Clubs

Unaffiliated clubs are local organizations. Any local group that is not a part of a larger national organization is an unaffiliated club. The Rotary, Jaycees, Lions, and so on are part of large national organizations so they are affiliated organizations.

Your fear of speaking vanishes if you start at the lowest rungs on the speaking ladder where speaking is easy.

They are the key for beginning speakers. These speaking engagements are easy to get. You do not have to invest a lot of time and effort in preparing to speak at them. These groups are casual and not intimidating. You are really chatting, not making a speech. If you stumble, mumble, and bumble, no one is going to be very critical. By speaking to them over and over, you learn not to stumble, mumble, and bumble.

Speaking to these groups can get you known in the local market. These groups can win you customers. Speaking to these groups leads inevitably to other speaking opportunities.

In other words, speaking at this level has no risk and it is always rewarding.

Unaffiliated organizations include your local pet clubs, charity groups, PTAs, hospitals, cancer support groups, bicycle clubs, garden clubs, historical societies, tax payers leagues, athletic organizations, local television stations, newspapers, radio shows that sponsor charity events, and so on. The list is virtually endless. Some of these groups meet weekly. Others meet monthly. Some meet irregularly. Some are only once a year.

You move up to more and more valuable and lucrative speaking events one easy step at a time.

In larger cities, some of these local groups are very large, and very well established. Some are also very prestigious, with histories going back decades, but most are small and very local. Every city and town has a variety of clubs that meet to discuss various topics for a variety of reasons. You can pick and choose which groups to address based upon your topic.

In many cases, your topic points clearly to which of these groups you want to address. For example, a friend, Steven Cordell, owns the Steve Cole Salon in Seattle. He was shy about speaking but wanted to get his salon better known. After we discussed speaking, he realized that there were lots of small local women's groups that he could address. Once he realized who his audience was, speaking was less frightening. After all, as a hairdresser, he spent all day every day talking to women.

For someone like Steven, the groups represent his customer base, but even if these groups aren't your target customers, you start here because it is the best possible training ground for speaking.

These groups are visible because they are always looking for new members. If you go to your local library—or other local libraries—and the chamber of commerce, they will usually have lists of these local organizations. You will sometimes find them in the yellow pages or see them advertised on community bulletin boards at your local supermarket. Local hobby shops, pet stores, and garden stores can connect you to groups of hobbyists, pet owners, and garden clubs.

You can also contact local restaurants and hotels that offer meeting space. They can often put you in touch with the meeting coordinators who use their space.

To get invited to speak at unaffiliated clubs, you just call the meeting coordinator. These groups are always looking for new, interesting speakers. They get a lot of their local real estate people, tax planners, and insurance salespeople. You stand out from the crowd if you aren't selling what they are tired of hearing about.

If you are a local businessperson selling to the public, these people are your customers. You make money by getting yourself known to them and helping them. People do business with people they know and like.

You cannot usually sell at the meetings, but you can often use these groups to help you sell your products, especially if you have traditional speakers' products. One of the best ways is

KEY STEPS

by helping these groups with fund-raising.

None of these groups pay speakers fees beyond a free meal. The people who attend these meetings will buy few books or other materials. However, these groups need to raise money at various times for various reasons. If you make a good impression on them, you can get invited back and develop relationships with them. You can then sell your product by helping them raise money and make money yourself in the process.

They can promote a presentation given by you, charging a fee to people who attend. The organization sells tickets (for $25 each, for example) to raise funds. You can give its members and their families a discount and charge full price to nonmembers. The organization arranges the meeting space, refreshments, advertising, mailing list, postage, printing, and labor. You give the talk. You then split the gate 50/50 with them. They make money and so do you.

You don't even have to charge a fee once you are confident of your ability to speak and promote your product. You propose a fund-raising event in which you give a presentation for a larger group or the general public. The group publicizes and organizes the free event, getting a good-sized audience. You use the event to make your presentation, get the group excited, and sell your product—for example, books, tapes, and so on, and you then DONATE 20–25 percent of the proceeds to the organization. You can make up to $2,000 per event, depending on your products.

As you work with these groups, you will discover a variety of other opportunities for making money. The contacts you make within them lead to other speaking opportunities. People who are part of one group are many times more likely than the average person to be part of another group. This is where you start to build the network of contacts that is so important to good strategy.

Speaking to these unaffiliated groups leads naturally to the next rung on the speaking ladder, the affiliated organizations.

Affiliated Organizations

Affiliated organizations all belong to a national network of local groups that have regular meetings. Every community has it local Rotaries, Lions, Jaycees, parent/teacher organizations, chambers of commerce, and so on.

These groups offer many of the advantages of unaffiliated clubs, but they also offer their own unique advantages. Speaking opportunities are easy to get. You still do not have to invest effort in preparing to speak. Though you need to be more polished as a speaker, the environment is still casual.

More importantly, your success with one chapter leads directly to speaking opportunities at other chapters. These groups help spread the word about you, and most connect you with the local business community. Their members include influential members of the local community. These groups are well known, and references from them give you the credibility you need to take the next step.

Speaking to local Rotaries, Jaycees, and similar groups puts you into the local network of decision-makers.

Most of these groups meet more often and more regularly than unaffiliated groups. Most are organized around meal meetings, usually lunch. At the end of the meal, you get up for only about twenty minutes and talk.

Another advantage of these groups is that they are usually

much more visible than unaffiliated clubs. They are larger, better known, better organized, better financed, and more actively looking for members.

Again, go to your local library (or different local libraries) and the chamber of commerce. Libraries will always have contact information for these local organizations. However, many (though not all) of these organizations are in the phone book. In most cases, you can contact their national headquarters and get contact information for the local branches. On our money-speaking.com web site, we offer links to many of these organizations for our registered owners of this book.

To get invited to speak, you call the meeting coordinator. Some of these groups have so many speakers, that the meeting coordinator changes from month to month. The standards of these groups are a little higher and that makes their job that much more difficult. They insist that speakers present on topics of general interest. You can't just give sales pitches.

Speaking to well-known local organizations makes you credible and connects you to members of the community.

Fund-raising is even more important for these groups. Many of these groups exist primarily as charitable organizations. Many may be open to new fund-raising ideas such as a paid or free lecture, but many will have long-established fund-raising events that you can take part in.

These fund-raising events are long established and well promoted. You want to take part in them if you can. Many of these events will allow you to work in your presentation or sell your product if you split the proceeds with the charity. Since many of the members of these organizations are shy about speaking themselves, their events may require an outside host or moderator. These positions also give you an opportunity to get better known.

The biggest opportunity with these groups is the connections they offer. They are your best introduction to the important organizations in your local community. They give you the opportunity to meet and get to know the people who run local businesses, associations, charities, local politicians, and government offices.

These affiliated organizations are a key link to moving up to the next and most lucrative rung on the speaking ladder.

Local Businesses and Other Organizations

You should care about this group because, as Willie Sutton is famous for explaining, this is where the money is. For most spokespeople, local businesses and organizations are the main source of income. They control a vast amout of money and have a lot of needs.

There are over 14 million small businesses in America. Politicians and the news media focus on big corporations, but 80 percent of the population is employed in local businesses. Every industry and profession, from accountants to zoologists, has local associations. Even big corporations, big unions, big government, and big charities exist and spend primarily as local, independent branches.

It doesn't matter where you live or what your topic is—there are thousands of these organizations in your area. All of them have meetings. All of them need training. Most of them pay for ideas. Make no mistake about it: this is where the money is. You may want to climb higher on the speaking ladder to reach your goals, but this is as high as you need to get to make your efforts start paying for themselves.

These organizations need speakers. The best opportunities in this market take three forms: 1) sales and marketing training, 2) management training, and 3) organization meetings.

Sales and marketing training is vital because those activities generate money for the organization. Sales departments always have a training budget. Management training is common, especially in government offices and local divisions of larger organizations. Organizations as small as a few dozen employees have annual meetings. The larger the local organization, the more often it meets and the more types of meetings it has.

This is the first level at which you can get paid speakers fees and training fees. This is where your speaking and training products can really make money. It is also important for selling any type of consulting.

These local engagements are also a vital step in proving the value of your products and building your credibility. The programs you develop working with these local organizations are identical to the programs you offer at the highest levels of speaking.

Local branches of large, well-known organizations are especially valuable to those starting out in speaking because you get the credibility of adding their well-known names to your list of clients and contacts.

The challenge isn't finding these organizations. You can just open the yellow pages and find thousands of them. The challenge is that none of them will want to talk to you. They have all kinds of people calling them trying to sell them products and services.

You need to find the right organizations, the ones that will find your topic most valuable. The next challenge is getting in contact with a decision-maker who will invite you to speak. The easiest way to contact these groups is by using the previous rung on the speaking ladder as your introduction. Initially, the best way to make contacts is by speaking at local affiliated organizations. These speaking engagements get you in front of these decision-makers. This is why it is so important to polish your presentations before working with affiliates. You need the people who hear you to want more of you.

If you do a good job at the affiliate level, you meet the decision-makers at this level. This gets you inside the very special world of local business owners, branch managers, and department heads.

Once you are inside this world, you become part of a network of contacts. You know people who know people. You ask for a reference from one person who has invited you to speak to other people like himself or herself. These connections are endless.

Your network of local business contacts is an invaluable resource in making you successful as a spokesperson.

You must actively build and use your contacts to get invited to speak to local organizations. At the end of a presentation to any group, you must make it clear that you are available to speak and train local organizations. When networking at the end of these meetings, you collect cards and contact names.

If your contact doesn't hire speakers and trainers directly, you can ask for the name and contact information of the person in that individual's organization who does. You then send that person information to introduce yourself. In your letter, you want to start with who referred you to them. You then follow up on that letter with a call to arrange a personal interview.

You get these jobs by sitting down with the decision-maker and discussing what you can do for his or her organization. If there is a committee involved, you ask for half an hour to give a part of your presentation. At this meeting, you explain how your speaking can help them become more competitive as a business and make more money.

Your ability to make money at this level depends largely on your assets and products. I started giving seminars for local businesses when personal computers were first introduced. I gave the seminars for free but I made money by selling computers. Because I was out there speaking about the new generation of computers, I was quickly promoted from sales to management to national accounts marketing within two years.

Of the forty billion dollars spent annually on business training, 80 percent is spent at the local level.

For traditional speakers payment is direct. You charge these companies for hiring you. Price depends on the size and budget of the companies and upon your resume in training businesses. Generally a few hundred dollars for a presentation is a good starting point. You can discount based upon how badly you need the experience and by how valuable the organization's reference will be to other similar businesses.

You should be willing to speak to any local trade association meeting for free. For example, the American Management Association breakfast meetings to start the day for managers around the country. There are a number of such management groups that regularly bring decision-makers together for educational purposes. These organizations will buy your other products more or less automatically when you get them into your customer funnel. In other cases, you can sell those products to their employees. In some cases, you can partner with them to introduce their products and your own to their customers.

Remember that a specific industry focus is more valuable. You can follow your contacts deeper into a specific industry. For example, a talk at one branch of a bank leads to more talks at other branches of the same bank. This leads you to talking at other local banks and their branches. This vertical focus deepens and broadens your understanding of the problems and needs within the industry. Through speaking, you learn the industry and turn a low-priced generic form of expertise into a high-priced industry-specific one. The most valuable experts are those who can connect their knowledge with the everyday needs of specific groups of people.

Colleges and Educational Institutions

Every community has educational institutions that offer adult education courses. For more and more of these organizations, adult education is a vital part of their income stream. They rely heavily on bringing in outside experts from their community to provide these adult education courses. These experts offer courses in everything from tai chi to tax planning.

You can get experience, gain credibility, and make money speaking for these organizations. What gives you more credibility than being able to say, "I teach at a college"? You also make contact with local businesspeople who are taking these courses for self-improvement.

Getting the opportunity to offer an adult education course

is easier than you might imagine. You make contact with the organizations and find out about the adult education programs and which topics they prefer. You get their course lists to see what they offer, who is teaching the courses, and what they are charging. You can then contact some of the teachers to learn about how they got hired.

Most institutions require you to submit a written proposal for the course. They need to know its length, what you will charge for teaching it, the number of students in the class, and so on. They may offer examples of these proposals and provide guidelines for submission. However, before you offer a proposal, you need to use your contact with the other teachers to tell you what the institution is really looking for, especially in terms of what fees are possible. Every college has different preferences.

Some colleges also use "circuit speakers," who are not local presenters. Usually getting hired to present a lecture series involves a different group of decision-makers. Many rely on showcases, which we discuss later, to choose lecturers.

How much money you can make depends on the institution, but the pay is not great. Some will pay a set fee. Others give you a percentage based on how much they bring in from your course or seminar. Some also offer "free seminars" where they either charge you for the room and promoting the event or split the proceeds from product sales. However, if you can develop close relationships with your students the opportunities can lead to long-term sales.

Credentials from an educational organization are useful but not essential to making the next step up to speaking at local conventions and meetings.

Local Conventions and Visitors' Bureaus

Local convention centers, hotels that host conventions, and visitors' bureaus exist to promote their facilities for conventions. Visitors' bureaus are often voluntary organizations, though in larger cities and states they are regular government offices. Hotels have paid sales departments. Large convention centers and meeting venues such as sport facilities can have their own similar sales organizations. These organizations provide services for events, including referring local speakers to events planners coming into town. They also organize local events.

These organizations can always refer you to event organizers. Sometimes they are event organizers. These groups are local so you do not have to travel to get in front of large national groups. If you develop a track record with these local organizations, they will give you more business.

You find these groups by looking under "convention and meeting facilities" in your local phone book for smaller ones. At www.money-speaking.com, we publish a list of the major state and city organizations with links for our registered book owners.

Local convention centers give you exposure to nationwide events and bigger audiences without leaving home.

You work with these organizations much like you work with an event promoter, which we explain in detail in the next section. After all, these organizations sometimes are event promoters. You sometimes have to join the local chamber of commerce or similar groups to work with these organizations, which can cost $400 or so, but you can sometimes get fees waived.

Your big advantage in working with these groups is that you are local. At every big convention, a few scheduled speakers cancel their plans to speak at the last minute. The event organizer only has time to bring in a local replacement. These organizations have files of information on local speakers just for this purpose.

Offer your presentation for free to the convention and visitors' committee members or members of the local chamber if it controls the group. These organizations can recommend you to the organizers with whom they are working if you treat the event coordinators in the organization well. You can get to know these individuals and develop relationships when you are hired by local businesses that are working with them.

Many of these convention organizations offer regular home shows or business expos at which you can speak, though frequently you pay for the room. Do not trust the event organizers to draw a crowd for you at these events. Attendance can vary dramatically from year to year depending on how well the events are publicized. These events can offer opportunities to start promoting your own public seminars at a reasonable price.

Speaking at local nationwide meetings qualifies you to move up to travel to nationwide meetings anywhere.

Working at this local level is your natural entry to working with national seminar and event promoters.

Seminar and Event Promoters

This moves you to speaking on a nationwide stage. Seminars, conventions, and trade meetings are promoted every day in every city in America. Most are regional or national meetings for specific industries, professions, or interests. Still others are on specific topics such as marketing. Still others are for the general public teaching them how to become entrepreneurs, get out of debt, lose weight, find romance, or start some type of business. Still others offer several-day workshops on any of these topics.

This is the heart of the business for professional speakers. Because of that, there is more competition at this level. You need to be very confident in your abilities, the quality of your materials, and your ability to sell before you step up to this level. These event promoters are in business for one reason: to make money. It doesn't matter if the event is put on by a regional trade organization or a for-profit seminar group—all of them are about making money. Do not move up to this market until you are confident in your ability to make sales.

All these organizations use their events as a way to connect buyers and sellers. They make money by charging the sellers promotional fees to access their community. They charge vendors for booth space at trade meetings. They also charge vendors for advertising at their events. If you are categorized as a vendor in their minds, they will want to charge you.

However, if you position yourself as a polished, professional expert, they can pay you. These promoters offer education programs as part of the fee they charge attendees. They look for interesting new content to attract attendees. If you get accepted into the promoter's event circuit, you can build up credentials as an attraction. If you can make money for these promoters, your future as a spokesperson is assured.

You will find it easier to get accepted on a national level if you develop your expertise within a vertical market, that is, in a specific industry, profession, or any area of interest that has regular meetings. For example, the Science of Strategy Institute looks for spokespeople to work in the martial arts marketplace as an interest group outside of business that uses our materials and has regular meetings across the nation.

The easiest way to find out about these events is from your connections in your local market. Your contacts with local meeting planners lead to national contacts. Your local business contacts can tell you about the events, conferences, conventions, and meetings in their industry. Even with just one customer in an industry, you can get a connection to an event planner. If you develop a presentation for that specific industry, you have a natural entrée.

You can also check trade and special interest magazines for events and seminars being offered in various vertical markets. You should also check "entrepreneur" magazines and start with those offering seminar programs in your area.

To get invited to speak, you must first understand the event promoters' revenue model. Do they pay speakers? Do they expect people to speak for free? Do they share revenue with speakers? Do they charge speakers for room time and equipment? Do they require speakers to buy a booth? All these models are used. You don't know what model a given promoter uses until you ask. At any given event, more than one model can be used. Speakers in the general session might be paid, but speakers in the breakout rooms might present for free, selling their products or services, or perhaps paying for their room or splitting sales with the promoter.

You start by asking the promoter how he or she operates, but you also want to check with a few speakers who have worked the events. Obtain a past or future brochure for the event and get the speakers' names. Search for them on the web and give them a call and ask about the event. Contact more than one type of speaker to get an idea.

The next step is sending a letter—not e-mail—and an information package to the promoter introducing yourself. You must make it clear why people at the event would find your presentation interesting, and how it is different and more interesting than what most speakers offer. You must emphasize the number of talks you have given, but only name organizations—such as businesses, colleges, local events—that relate in some way to the targeted event. Speaking to unaffiliated and affiliated organizations gives you little credibility with most promoters.

More and more event organizers make money from splitting product sales with these speakers. The speakers who make this work are those who know how to present their products so that the entire audience gets good value out of the presentation and enough of the audience buys the speaker's product to make it worth the speaker's time. The event promoters who make this work are selective about the speakers they hire.

As a multibillion dollar business, the meeting and convention business depends on new ways of making money.

The term "conversion ratio" is used to describe how good a speaker is at turning audience members into buyers. If half of the audience buys, your conversion ratio is 50 percent. You and the promoter can calculate what a given audience is worth by multiplying the audience size times your conversion ratio for that type of audience. If you don't have enough experience to know, be honest about it. You want your results to exceed expectations rather than disappoint.

For promoters who share in product sales, you must make the case for working with you in dollars and cents. Don't be shy about making it clear that you too are focused on making sales to your audience. All event promoters are in business to make money. Your seminars must generate money for the seminar promoter.

Initially, you must be willing to accept a breakout session room for a concurrent session. Do well there and you can get invited to speak at the main session, addressing all attendees. I spoke at these events in the computer industry for years. I started in breakout rooms, then graduated to main sessions, and then became an expert used on panels. I spoke for free, and the result was that we built one of the Inc. 500 fastest-growing companies in America.

When I started speaking about strategy, I started getting invited to a broader range of events. These events took me all over the world. After I sold my software company, I kept getting invited to these events on the basis of my reputation, but since I didn't have a product to sell when I started, I began charging speaking fees.

Speaking at international conventions and meetings exposes you to the very highest level of contacts in the world.

You can make money at these events in many different ways. At first, you might speak for free just to get the experience and references. Then you can start selling your products at the back of the room and either keeping all the money or splitting it with the seminar promoter. Speaking for a fee can actually be less profitable than selling products at a big event because when you take a fee you cannot usually directly promote products.

Your Own Public Seminars

There are four steps to making your own public seminars a success. First, you have to know how to promote it to a local target market. Today, this is mostly a matter of having a great e-mail list for your local market. Second, you must know how to give a great seminar. Third, you must have products and know you can get people to buy your products by speaking to them. You should prove that you can sell at the event promoter level before you consider giving you own seminars. Finally, you need enough of a business operation so that after the seminar you can keep in contact with attendees and keep them moving through your product pipeline.

It helps if you know something about publicity and understand advertising. The real key here is having a great database. You can use in-house lists of previous customers, buy local lists, or split the seminar sign-up fees with those who have their own opt-in e-mail lists. You can also use your contacts with various affiliated and unaffiliated clubs to fill up a room.

If you master the art of producing your own seminars, you can become an event promoter yourself. You can start working with other speakers, bringing them into your events and splitting product sales while having them do the work.

To create these events, you have to be willing to take a financial risk. You need a topic you are certain will draw a crowd. You need to have the courage to make the investment. You must minimize your risks in this type of new venture. You start small, testing your concept in a limited way. It is much better to have a small seminar in a small room and turn away attendees than to have a large, empty room for which you are paying.

KEY STEPS

Rooms at hotels, convention centers and restaurants cost as much as several hundred dollars per day. Catering and equipment can run as much as another thousand. Sometimes hotels will give you the room for free in a hotel if you use their catering service. This seems like a win-win, but hotels charge a fortune for food. Always buy your coffee by the gallon, not by the cup.

At first, you must use free methods: publicity and joint ventures with local organizations. Publicity on local radio is especially important, but you can get free publicity in local papers as well. If you develop a track record that shows that this method works in your market, you may be able to afford advertising these events.

You can also arrange partnerships with local businesses, such as real estate agencies, that might have large mailing lists and want to get a crowd of people together.

You start with e-mail lists. For e-mail, you send out a message that links to a web site. If your concept works well, you can see whether direct mail pieces justify their extra cost. For physical mailing lists, your flyer should be a four-page self-mailer. Avoid radio and television advertising unless you attract the broadest audiences.

You make money through registration fees, immediate product sales, continued product sales, and by getting more work. Registration fees can range from free (to get a volume of people into your funnel) to over several hundred dollars per attendee (to create a sense of value). It is better to have either a free event or a high-priced event. People show up for free events or expensive events but tend to get sidetracked from mid-priced events. The higher the registration fee, the more you invest in marketing and the longer your time frames for getting registration. The more vertical your topic, the higher the price you can charge.

The Corporate Marketplace

While getting speaking opportunities at local departments of large companies is fairly easy, speaking at larger corporate meetings is more complicated. Many groups within a larger corporation set up the organization's meetings. The larger the division, the more professional the events are, including the use of specialized internal or external meeting planners.

Corporations pay you to speak. They pay you to train, frequently on a per diem basis. They can buy your products for their employees and customers. They give you credibility. They can buy consulting. They can engage you for numerous events.

Speakers of all types, depending on the level of hiring, can be invited, but fees are usually at least a few thousand dollars. Speakers bureaus, covered at the end of this chapter, specialize in these events and their speakers usually charge a minimum of several thousand dollars.

By speaking at local corporate events and national conferences, you develop your corporate contacts.

Corporate presentations represent the highest level of speaking. A successful presentation to one group or division of a corporation can lead to speaking opportunities with more groups and divisions. You can even get invited to a company's hospitality events for its customers, clients, or business partners. These presentations can take place at trade shows or in local offices.

Corporations are everywhere. You can work your way up from local divisions, though frequently the national organizations don't show much respect for their local branches. You can make more corporate contacts by working your national convention contacts and, of course, through speakers bureaus.

To get invited, you often need to impress the corporation's executives. They need to hear you speak at other conferences or read one of your books. The meeting planners hire whoever the executives want. Executives will like you if you combine knowledge of your topic with knowledge of their industry. They might want to use your expertise to draw in prospective clients or sell customers on a particular type of product.

In large corporations, budgetary authority is important. One firm rule is that sales and marketing are where the money is. Headquarters and executive staffs always have budgets as well. Groups such as human resources and employee training are more difficult in terms of limited budgets, especially at a group or departmental level.

Speaking to these groups is a key step, getting you out in front of people and polishing presentation skills.

Sales and marketing events pay the best. If you are giving a main session presentation for corporate customers, you can also offer advanced training for special customers at the event.

If a corporation has regular employee training events, you can help defray their costs by offering your seminar for free if they let you sell your products to employees. This should be presented as a win-win opportunity for you and the company. The company gets valuable free training and employees become even better trained on their own.

Other Ways to Get Audiences

Climbing these eight steps is the best way to find your audiences. However, there are two other ways you can get hired to speak. I haven't used them personally and don't necessarily recommend them, but you should know about them. They may work well for you given the right topic and situation.

Showcases

Showcases charge speakers a fee to present 10 minutes of their material for an audience of "speakers' circuit" promoters. It is basically a cattle call but some organizations only book speakers this way. Buyers and agents come to showcases to look, listen, and book speakers. When you pay your fee, you also get your name in the showcases catalog, which gets mailed out to those who book speakers.

The quality of showcases varies dramatically and since you have to invest in them and travel to them, they can be costly and risky. Most promoters who organize lecture series for colleges and high schools use showcases to find speakers. Some promoters for business events do as well. Some showcases are attended by speakers agencies and agents. I personally have never attended a speakers showcase though I have attended a publicity showcase. Most of the professional speakers I know consider showcases poor investments.

Showcases are easy to find. The National Association of Campus Activities (NACA), Meeting Professionals International (MPI), the American Society of Association Executives (ASAE), and the International Group of Agencies and Bureaus (IGAB) all offer showcases. You can also do a web search. Showcases also advertise to attract speakers. They exist to collect fees from would-be speakers.

Speakers Bureaus and Agents

These groups promote speakers. They work only with speakers who speak for a fee. They take a percentage of your speaking fee for booking you. Larger organizations go to bureaus to find speakers when they are looking for them.

At our web site, moneyspeaking.com, we offer a list of many of these bureaus for those who own this book. Your expertise and presentation must be suited for speaking for a fee. To get registered with these bureaus, you usually need an interesting topic (the more focused the better), a list of good references, a demonstration video, a four-color brochure that the organization can sell from, and a minimum charge of $3,000 per speech.

These organizations are not very selective. A single bureau can list tens of thousands of speakers. The problem here is standing out from the crowd. A unique topic and rave reviews from audiences cannot hurt, but bureaus only get close to a relatively few speakers. You can make a lot of money if you become a bureau favorite that they recommend to everyone.

The only downside to getting listed is that you have to pay the cost of creating marketing materials and your video. In return, you do get a higher than average fee less the commission charged by the agent or bureau. This commission runs from 15 to 30 percent.

Bureaus especially will offer you a lot of marketing "opportunities," which are generally a waste of money. I advise against joining a bureau that requires marketing fees up front, as some do. They simply don't pay for most speakers.

A Few Final Thoughts on These Key Steps

You move up the ladder of speaking venues one rung at a time. Each rung gives you the experience, material, and expertise to move to the next.

You speak at unaffiliated cubs to get comfortable speaking in a fail-proof environment and to make contacts in the community.

You speak at affiliated organizations to make money by sharing revenue with charities and to make business contacts.

You speak at local businesses and other organizations because that is where the money is.

You speak at colleges and other educational institutions to develop your material and give yourself more credibility.

You develop contacts with local convention centers and visitors' bureaus to break into national events.

You work with national seminar and event promoters to get access to large, successful audiences.

You promote your own public seminars when you know you have a topic that is appealing and your have products that you know will sell.

Speaking opportunities at every level can make you money as long as you adapt your product to the group.

You break into the corporate marketplace to get the biggest fees and every other form of income.

You pay to get to speakers showcases when you don't know how else to break into the speaking business.

You sign up with speakers bureaus and agents if you are certain you can stand out from the crowd.

CHAPTER 6

INFLUENCE
BY DESIGN

Your Presentation Strategy:
From Surprise to Action

The presentation template in this chapter is available no where else in the world. It is based upon analysis of the presentations made by the most successful speakers in the world.

Good speakers educate or motivate, but great spokespeople speak for one reason only: to get their audiences to take action. You design your presentations with this single goal in mind. There is a well-defined formula that the most influential speakers use to present their ideas to get their audiences to act.

In this chapter, you learn a powerful template for creating winning presentations. Once you learn this method, you will recognize its components whenever you listen to a successful speaker. Your passion, your expertise, and your sales assets all play a major role in this template, which is why we spent time discussing them. Your own presentations must be designed around your own life story and product, but the psychology of influence used in this template works for any story and any product.

The Keys to Influence

Influence comes from both technique and structure. You use psychological techniques to keep your audience involved in your presentation. You use a persuasive structure to lead listeners emotionally—and maybe even logically—to do what you are asking of them. The speaking techniques are simple to explain, but they require planning, practice, and courage to execute. The structure requires a great deal of explanation, but it is easy to implement.

Speaking Techniques

Great presentations have a special feel to them. As an audience member, you know when something out of the ordinary is happening. You recognize a great performance even when you are not otherwise interested in the topic. A great performance isn't a matter of having a great voice or a fluent speaking style. There are only three special techniques that you need to master to impress an audience: 1) getting reactions, 2) using repetition, and 3) contrasting variations in pattern, sound, and content.

Reaction

When you speak, you must get the audience to react. They must become part of the show. Every few minutes you must ask the audience a question, make them laugh, give them something to do, or surprise them. Emotion is the key to generating actions, but actions are the keys to emotion. If people are sitting passively and just listening, they will not get emotionally involved and you cannot persuade them to act.

> *Creating audience excitement when you speak has more to do with how you say it than what you actually say.*

I
N
F
L
U
E
N
C
E

It can be difficult to get audience reactions at first, but when you force audiences to react, the climate in the room changes. Everyone realizes that it is OK to react. Even a sprinkling of laughs tells everyone that it is OK to laugh. Then more people join in. People begin to relax and enjoy themselves. You have to keep involving the audience throughout the presentation, and you have to set the tone right from the beginning. You don't want them to feel pressure, but you must start by luring audiences into responding to what you are saying and doing.

Repetition

You must repeat your key messages and ideas in the same words and phrases, over and over again, to drive them home. You put these words into different contexts so that they take on different shades of meaning, but you use repetition.

Effective repetition is divided into two parts, the setup and the response phrases. From the setup phrase, your audience learns to expect the response to follow. You repeat this combination four or more times, emphasizing and exaggerating the setup and response phrases so the audience cannot help but notice them. The audience quickly learns what to expect. When you just say the setup phrase, you trigger the response phrase in audience members' minds without even saying it.

The techniques of reaction, repetition, and variation multiply their effects when they are combined.

Say you want to implant the response phrase "you must learn [your message]" in your audience's mind. You can set up this phrase by saying, "I don't want you to listen to [variation]," where the variation gives the phrase a slightly different meaning. For example, you might say, *"I don't want you to listen to* me talk. <u>*You*</u> *must learn* the spokesperson strategy." A little later, you say, "*I don't want you to listen to* what other people say. <u>*You*</u> *must learn* the spokesperson strategy." By the time you use the "*I don't want you to listen to...*" phrase the third time, the words "<u>*you*</u> *must learn*" will trigger the audience thinking "the spokesperson strategy."

When you combine reaction with repetition, the two techniques multiply the psychological involvement of the audience. By the third repetition, your audience is only thinking your response phrase, but if you encourage them, they will repeat the phrase with you. Then you can use your setup phrase and just gesture to the audience and they will say the response phrase for you. This is how you train an audience.

Variation

Repetition creates expectations. These expectations set up the final psychological technique, variation. A great presentation gains power not by constant pressure but by constant change. You create tension and suspense and then you release it. You speed up, then slow down, and then pause. You build up points and pound them home, faster and faster. Then you stop, step back, break the pace, and make a self-deprecating remark to let the audience take a breath.

The enemy is boredom and predictability. A voice is never boring as long as it changes pace, volume, and pitch. A story is never boring as long as it creates expectations, satisfies them, sets up more expectations, and then surprises you by changing directions. You use repetition to create a pattern, and then you break that pattern to call attention to a new idea. It almost doesn't matter what the variation is as long as the audience is continually getting something new and unexpected.

The Structure of a Presentation

You must take the audience through four steps to persuade them. Each of these four sections is necessary. You cannot skip one and convince your audience. First, you use the opening to grab the audience's attention and prepare them. Next the problem section proves their current perspective wrong. Then your lesson section gives them a new perspective. Finally, the decision section gets them to act.

The opening sets up the presentation by getting the audience immediately interested and preparing them for what value they should expect to get from listening to your talk.

The problem section establishes the need and value of what you want the audience to do. In this section, you raise the audience's objections and answer them. People have to know there is a problem before they are prepared to learn something new.

The lesson section introduces the audience to ideas that they did not know, but that they can easily accept as true. The lesson explains why the problem exists and what you need to do about it.

The decision section is designed to get the audience to act on an opportunity. You present them with an offer that is too good for them to pass up. You close the deal not just by telling them what you have to offer, but by giving them a decision that they have to make right now. The closing is the most important part of the presentation, but you never get there unless you do everything else right.

This format works for presentations from 20 minutes to

90 minutes long. The opening and the final decision sections each take about 10 percent of your presentation time, between two minutes and ten minutes each. The problem and lesson sections each take about 40 percent of the presentation, between eight and twenty-four minutes each. For longer presentations, you just repeat this same structure over and over.

The Opening: Start With a Blast!

Most people giving a presentation lose the audience in the first few seconds because they get started on the wrong note. Instead of getting people excited, they conform to the conventional niceties. This tells the audience that they are about to hear the same stuff that they have heard a thousand times before. Because the opening is so important, we discuss it in more detail than any other part of the presentation.

As a generation raised on television, your audience members have been conditioned to be passive, skeptical observers. The power of a live presentation is that the audience is part of the presentation. The purpose of the opening is to bring the audience into the moment. If you don't warm up the audience, they are going to sit there like lumps. If they sit through the presentation, they will sit at the end when you want them to act.

The first thirty seconds of your presentation determine whether or not your audience is really going to listen.

You set the tone from the first words out of your mouth. Don't thank everyone for coming, test the microphone, or pass out materials. Don't ask whether the audience can hear you. Don't start by saying anything they expect or have heard a million times before. Avoid phrases like "I am here today blah, blah, blah," where the "blah, blah, blah" is any polite and trite pronouncement of platitudes that we have all heard a million times.

If you say what is expected, you are dead. The audience will unconsciously start tuning you out. If you start talking without engaging your audience, you are dead. People are herd animals. If they see the others around them reacting, they are forced to react themselves. You use the audience to leverage your message. Their reactions and responses are the best live proof for what you are saying.

In the opening, you must do four things. First, you must say or do something unexpected and force the audience to respond. Next, you frame your presentation for the audience. Then you must recognize their skepticism and need for proof. Finally, you set the rules.

This is a lot to accomplish in the two to nine minutes you get for an opening. This means that this section must be the tightest and most carefully planned section of your talk. You never memorize your whole talk, but you want to have the first few minutes down cold. In this section, every paragraph, sentence, and word is important. You cannot waste any time because you don't have much time to win the audience.

Your opening requires the most planning before a presentation because it does so much groundwork.

Grab the Audience and Get a Response

Get the audience's attention and make them respond. You need to get them to sit up and take notice. It is easier if you accomplish your first two goals in one step. The best way to get attention is to elicit verbal or physical responses. Your audience members must hear and see other audience members responding. This forces them to join in the presentation and become part of it instead of being viewers.

To do this correctly, you want to: 1) do and say the unexpected, 2) ask questions to get the audience members thinking, and 3) demand a simple verbal or physical response. There are three common openings that accomplish these goals. There are many others, but these are easy to adapt to any topic.

The Surprising Question

Start with a question that is unexpected. The answer to this question should be obvious, but the question itself must get audience members thinking in a new way. For example, if you are addressing people in public service such as teachers or any profession that doesn't make a fortune, you can start with the question, "So since you are all teachers, most of you probably got into your profession to become millionaires, right?"

This gets a laugh, but then you can follow up with another question, "Oh, I have that wrong?" You then pause and wait for agreement from the audience.

If the audience is silent, don't be surprised. Whenever you ask the audience a question, getting that first response can be difficult. Here is a trick that always works. If you make eye contact with a specific audience member and ask that one person directly with a "can you help me here" version of the question, you will get a response. You can then ask the whole audience again, "We have someone who disagrees with me. What do you all think?"

When you get the audience going, you can then move on.

Ask, "Then what you are saying is that since you became teachers, you really don't care about money. That is too bad, because I have some lottery tickets here. One of them might be worth millions (hold up tickets). I was thinking about passing them out, but if no one here is interested in money that would be a waste of time wouldn't it?" This should get a reaction too. If it doesn't, ask, "Does anyone want one?" Ask again and again until hands are up all over. When the hands go up, you can say, "So you are interested in money. Now I am really confused."

You can then make the connection between your opening question and your topic. I used money in my example because money can be easily connected to so many topics.

Create the tension of unfinished business with your audience. For example, if you hold up the lottery tickets or any gift to get attention, you don't pass out them out—yet. It would be too distracting. But when you reveal any gift or prize, people expect you to give the gift right away. Keep the prize in plain site to let the tension build, but hold the gift until a transition point where you need the distraction and a change of pace.

This specific question about wanting to be a millionaire doesn't work if the audience is businesspeople. In that case, they expect the topic to be about money. Your question must be shocking. You have to come out of left field. For a business audience, you can try, "How many of you are professional criminals? Oh, I'm confused. Are you all amateurs then?" For most professions, you can say, "I really envy your profession. You work three hours a day, make six- to seven-figure annual salaries, take sixteen weeks of vacation and are totally free to do whatever you want." You pause for audience response and ask, "Oh, was I misinformed?"

The Problem Story

Another common way to grab an audience's attention is to start with a story that puts them into a scene where they have a serious problem. Tell your story in the second person, framing it so that they are forced to see themselves in that situation. The story has to be reasonable—something that they could see happening to themselves by some combination of circumstances. Ideally, it should be based on a true story. In your story, you make the situation worse and worse to build tension. As with any story, you offer as many specifics and details as you have time for, but here is a short example:

Example: "Your employee just stole $13,453. How do you feel? Everyone blames you. You are standing in front of a judge, and he sentences you to three years in prison. You say, 'I didn't do a thing.' But that is the problem, you didn't do a thing to prevent the situation. How many of you want to be in this situation?"

By telling this story, making it as specific and painful as possible, you are getting your audience emotionally involved in a new way. You get their imagination working, picturing a time and place that they didn't expect.

You can connect that problem situation with the need to learn your topic, but you can revisit this story throughout your presentation to develop your ideas and keep the audience involved not only at the beginning, but throughout the presentation.

These three example openings illustrate how much you can accomplish if you have a systematic approach.

As you go on, you can move from the second person to talking about a real person who you know. You develop the lead character and the plot to hold your audience in suspense. If you make the problem story come alive, your audience will want to know what happens to the people involved.

Mocking a Tepid Response

This opening works because audiences are always shy at the beginning of a talk unless they are drunk or another speaker has gotten them going. In these cases, this opening won't work. When you use this opening, you start with what looks like a boring opening and, when your audience reacts in a predictable way, you turn their reaction around on them.

You start by telling the audience that you are speaking to help them reach a goal. This goal must be as specific as you can make it for the audience members. For example, if you are addressing real estate agents, you can say, "I am here to help you sell one more house this week." For businesspeople, you can try, "I am here today to fill your wallets with money. Can I get an 'amen' to that?" For political candidates, you can say, "I am here today to get you all elected. How much do you want to get elected?"

In every opening, you have to prepare for the fact that, initially, your audience is not going to react.

When you first ask an audience anything, you get an anemic halfhearted response. Your audience members aren't prepared to get involved. You expect this response. This allows you to play up their response and make a point about how people attend meetings to help them reach their goals, but at the same time they are often too cynical about both reaching their goals and the speakers to get anything out of what they learn.

When the audience fails to react, you feign confusion and say. "Well, I'm sorry. I must be in the wrong place. Isn't this the [specific group you are addressing]? It is?" Here you look more confused and shrug, saying, "Let me start again."

The next step is to exaggerate your question, begging for a response. For example, you say, "I am here to fill your wallets with money—no, fill your bank accounts with money, so much money that your bank won't be able to hold it. Can I get an 'amen' to *that*?" You make eye contact with a few specific individuals in the audience as you ask. This will get you more of a response.

The audience will start to understand the game and play along. You repeat the exaggeration again and more people will join in. Your can keep exaggerating until you get everyone in the audience participating.

Frame Your Presentation for the Audience

Audiences come into the room with certain expectations. You have to start by disrupting those expectations. The first words out of your mouth must interrupt their pattern of thinking. You can then frame your presentation for them.

An initial surprise sets the theme for all that follows. People think they know is what going to happen. A surprising opening proves they don't. When you start correctly, the audience has to pay attention because they don't know where you are going. This is why people want surprises. They like being made to feel. You have to start with emotion to end with emotion.

You have already proven that they don't know what is going to happen, so you can now set their expectations correctly. This next part of your opening has four goals. First, you clarify what the audience will take away from your presentation. Next, you tell them they can get this information nowhere else. Then, you tell them how this information can change their lives. Finally, you let them know how long you will speak.

After opening with a surprise, your audience needs direction. You focus on their needs. You tell them that when they leave, they will be able to do things that they could not do before. What is your audience going to learn? They are going to learn about a secret formula that they can get nowhere else that will change their lives. You can communicate this message in several different ways in the three remaining sections of your presentation.

This is a place where you can insert your first repeated phrase. For example, you can say, "You will learn three things today." You then list those three, using the same setup phrase followed by the same response phrase. You list the three things they will learn as a variation of the setup phrase, followed by a response phrase emphasizing the value of the presentation.

Though too vague, a generic example might be to say, "First, I will shine a light on where we lose our way making it hard to discover a better life. Then I will shine a light on a new formula that enables you to discover a better life. Finally, I will shine a light on a program you can start today to discover a better life."

Your job in the opening is to create curiosity, interest, and excitement. Notice that in the example above, you don't tell people they will learn everything about your topic. They are going to learn *about* your system. In other words, you are going to describe the formula generally and tell them the next step in mastering it.

Recognize the Need for Proof

Since you have just made strong claims for your presentation, the natural reaction is skepticism. This skepticism can take many forms, but some of the most common skeptical reactions are the following:

"This has nothing to do with me."

"A lot of people make claims."

"I already understand about [your topic]."

"How do I know that any of this is true?"

At this point, you briefly acknowledge skepticism. You don't want to brand your audience as skeptics, but you make it clear that many people are. When you tell people not to do something, they naturally do it. So if you tell them, "Don't be skeptical," they will be skeptical. The right approach is to recognize that many people are skeptical and promise to address those natural doubts.

For example, you can say, "I hate it when people get in front of an audience and make a bunch of claims. I am not particularly skeptical, but anyone can claim that anything is true. I am not going to do that. I will have evidence for everything I say. I will give you evidence that this formula works. I will give you evidence that it helps people like you. Don't believe my claims; consider the evidence and see if it doesn't make sense."

Or you can say, "I am making big claims here. If I make big claims, you should expect me to prove them. You should demand that I prove them. As I talk, I am going to play the

> *You plug into what the audience is thinking and become their spokesperson when you play the role of the skeptic.*

INFLUENCE

121

skeptic for you. Whenever I ask, 'Why believe me?' I will speak for you and say, 'I demand proof!'" This version creates a new repeated phrase with its own setup and response.

Repeated phrases are especially good for calling attention to whatever logic, evidence, testimonials, or other proof you offer. You want this evidence to stand out in the presentation. In the end, people will not remember the evidence itself, but they will remember the repeated phrase calling attention to it.

The evidence you offer will always be more believable if you: 1) are very specific with all numbers and facts, and 2) paint detailed pictures of simple situations. The more specific you are, and the more detailed you are, the more people believe you.

Set the Rules

The opening is also when you can set some rules and expectations. First, you want to tell the audience how long you are talking. Then you want to tell them that there will be a break after your presentation. Next you need to explain how you want to handle questions. Finally, you want to tell them about notes or handouts.

You must first frustrate your audience's expectations because then you can create new ones.

The message here is that you have only a limited amount of time, and you want them to get the maximum return on that time. In short presentations, you want to discourage questions because you can get sidetracked. You don't want people worrying about handouts or taking notes. You want to keep attention focused on you and your presentation. At the very beginning, you want to make it clear that you are in control.

You need the audience to know how long you will talk and

that there will be a break afterward. You may have already told them how long you will be speaking, but they should also know that they will get a break after your presentation.

In short, tightly planned presentations, questions interrupt your flow and waste time. If you have designed your presentation correctly, you should answer all the audience's questions and objections in the course of the talk. Most questions address points you will raise later. Those who have enough courage to ask questions often want to argue or get attention for themselves.

Instead of saying, "No questions," you can say something like, "Please hold any question until the end." Or, if you pass out a sheet for recording feedback, "Please note any questions on the feedback sheet and I will collect them at the end." This gives people another reason to hand in their feedback sheets.

Handouts also detract from your presentation. People read them instead of listening. You want them to focus on what you are saying. Your message is reinforced if they take notes. At the end, you can use their desire for a copy of your information as another reason to give you a feedback sheet and their contact information.

For example, you can say, "I only have a few minutes here today. I want to fill it full of my best information for you. Because there is so much more to learn and because I am easily sidetracked I am going to ask you to hold your questions until the end. I will be here after the end of my talk and I promise to answer all your questions. You are going to want to take notes. I will be telling you a lot of things about [topic] that you simply cannot learn anywhere else."

This last step closes your few minutes of opening.

I
N
F
L
U
E
N
C
E

The Problem: Prove Their Assumptions Wrong

This is the first long section of your presentation. It lays the foundation for the lesson section. Here you make the case that people need to learn something. Since it is easier to find proof of problems than solutions, this section uses more proof than the next long section. The problem section has two parts. First, you list common mistaken assumptions and give evidence that proves them wrong. Then you tell your personal story.

There are eight common categories of mistaken assumptions that you can prove wrong. You do not have time to cover them all. You must pick the ones that build the strongest case for your particular topic and audience.

1. People think they don't need your ideas. Here you give examples of the costly and expensive decisions normal people have made because they didn't know what you are teaching. For example, in my presentations, I explain very briefly how John Kerry could have beaten George Bush if he had used the principles of strategy to craft a clear position on the war instead of simply attacking Bush. When I do, both Democrats and Republicans agree that Kerry probably would have won.

2. People think that your ideas are simplistic and that they can figure it out for themselves if they need to. Admit that people may eventually figure it out, but give examples that show that the delay will be extremely costly or the solution too late. I like to quote Gracian: "A wise man does at once what a fool does at last. Both do the same things only at different times."

3. People can think that the skills you teach are too complicated. You need to show that anyone can learn what you have to teach. It isn't complicated or difficult. It is just secret. You don't

have to study for years. You just need to know the secret.

4. People think that if what you teach were so valuable everyone would know it. Here you can admit that some lucky or smart people do figure it out, but say that your formula is sensitive. You need to get all the ingredients in the right proportion to get it to work well. That is why most people go wrong. They do almost everything right but miss an ingredient or two so they can't get it to work. You can give examples of complicated formulas that you could never get right, even knowing the ingredients. For example, "Even if you knew the ingredients for gunpowder, could you make it work?"

5. People can think that the skills you teach require special abilities. Here you give testimonials of ordinary people, with ordinary skills and weaknesses, who have been able to use the knowledge you provide. For the science of strategy, I give examples of people who I know who are teaching it to their children.

6. People think that learning your topic is more trouble and less rewarding than some alternative solution to the problem. To counter this idea, you discuss the alternatives. You purposely create a series of a "straw men" arguments knowing that you can knock them down. List alternatives and give examples of why they are more costly and less rewarding.

7. People think that they can learn your topic from other or less expensive sources. Here you need to explain why these alternatives don't work. You can offer a number of reasons, but by this time you should be able to refer to stories you have already told to show that this can't be true.

All people feel special so start by listing objections regular people have so your listeners can think they are different.

8. People like excuses to not take action. This leads logically from the last mistaken assumptions. For most people, reading a book is an excuse not to master a skill and to maintain their old habits. You take in some knowledge, but your habits remain the same. How many alcoholics are cured by reading book? This is a very good place to end this section because it sets up a key idea for your lesson. You can say, "Before you heard me speak, you had a great excuse for not learning about my topic. When we are done, I am not going to leave you any excuse for not taking action."

Providing Proof

During this section, you are going to give all kinds of proof. Since everyone needs proof, the emphasis in this section is on providing evidence that there is a need for mastering your topic.

You shouldn't make any point in this section unless you can also provide proof either from your own life or other sources. To establish proof, you need to present the information, and you have to tell the audience where you got the information and how it pertains to the point you are making. In other words, you have to make it clear. The point of offering proof is to knock down people's objections right and left.

The easiest and most believable evidence to provide to an audience is proof that a problem exists.

Proof is any of the following:

• Material you can hold up: articles from magazines and newspapers

• Facts and statistics you can cite

• Everyday examples you can give

• True anecdotes you can tell

- Pictures of people or situations, before and after
- Testimonials
- Stories about investing a little and getting a big return
- Any precise numbers, down to the smallest digit

The best proof is testimony that your audience itself can give to validate your points. When you say something, others will doubt you. When their fellow audience members say it, the rest of the audience believes it. When you get people trying to think of examples and proof themselves, they convince themselves. For example, if you want to prove that a situation is a common form of problem, ask the audience: "How many of you have been faced with this situation? Let me see your hands! How many of you responded this way? Let me see those hands!"

In a seminar on strategy for political candidates, I wanted to prove that most political campaign strategy missed the most basic issues, such as using readily available statistics. To prove my case, I asked, "How many of you know how many votes it took in the last election for the winner to get elected to the office you are running for?" Only one candidate out of more than thirty did. My point about holes in strategic knowledge needed no further proof.

You can reward those who get involved and offer proof. Incentives increase audience participation. If you introduced lottery tickets or other gifts in your opening, this is where you start passing them out. If you start rewarding people for getting involved, they will stay involved. When you reward an audience, do not give out samples of your product. If you do, you are giving the people you reward a reason not to take action at the end of the presentation: they will want to review what you gave them first. It not only hurts your closing, but it devalues what you are offering when you pass it out for free. Instead, give out neutral prizes, such as lottery tickets or even candy bars.

If your proof is extreme, people will think you are exaggerating. You prove you are not by going through the details.

You don't have to offer all your proof at once. You can save proof for later in the presentation to build up tension and suspense. For example, you can say, "I have a real concrete example of this later in my talk and I'll tell you in just a few minutes." This creates tension but if you make these promises you have to honor them.

Objections and Mistaken Assumptions

If people didn't naturally have false assumptions and make mistakes, there would be no need for the knowledge you are going to give them. This section is where you fulfill your promise made in the opening to address the skeptics in the audience and prove there is a problem.

In this section, you are really handling people's objections to learning what it is you are going to tell them. This gives you the opportunity to tell a lot of vivid stories about the mistakes you and others you know have made. This should be fast paced with the most audience involvement. Keep asking questions. Get hands raising. Get people repeating phrases with you. Ask audience members to read articles, testimonials, and other material for you. Keep it moving and keep them involved.

Rapid-Fire Lists

One of the common ways to handle this section is to go rapidly through mountains of issues and lots of evidence. Lists can be boring, so you must make this the most fast-paced—even frenetic—part of your presentation. You list problems. You offer evidence. You keep moving from one point to the next. The goal is to create a mountain of proof that there is a problem. This means coming at the problem from as many different directions as possible.

The Story Approach: Your Friend, the Skeptic

Instead of listing mistaken assumptions and objections, you can turn them into a story. You can personify the skepticism of the audience by telling the story of a friend of yours who is a confirmed skeptic and critic. You can bring out a series of objections but put them in the mouth of this friend. You can even make this "friend" your own mother or father-in-law, since these people are known to be skeptical. You can use real-life examples of a series of skeptics that you have personally faced and then put them into a single fictitious character.

You then use this character to raise objection after objection. You tell the story of this skeptic and how he or she criticized some aspect of your strategic formula. After you proved or the individual discovered that he or she was wrong, he or she raised another criticism. When that was proven wrong, the individual raised another. In the course of telling this story, you illustrate the thinking of a skeptic, proving it wrong in a way that gets the audience rooting for you against the skeptic. This story has a happy ending when after seeing the results with his or her own eyes, the skeptic is converted.

For an audience, vivid stories are more persuasive proof than hard evidence or any form of tightly reasoned abstract logic.

Your Personal Story

Your own life story is the only piece of proof you must offer an audience. You tell your story after you provide objective proof. Here you make the proof more intimate and personal. Remember, the goal of this seminar is to make the audience want more of you. This means you must talk about yourself and your history. It means exposing your flaws and getting the audience involved in the journey that you have taken.

This doesn't take much time. Many speakers spend more time on their personal story than is productive. As critical as it is, nobody wants to know your story beyond ten minutes, which is all the time you spend in a ninety-minute presentation. In a twenty-minute presentation, you can cut that back to two minutes. You want to come across as a regular person. You must admit your weaknesses, mistakes, and defects. You want to build yourself up only in ways that relate specifically to your expertise.

Your life story should say the following:

- I tried this idea and it worked.

- I shared it with my friends and it worked for them.

Since people are taking their time to listen to you, they want to know how you are special and different.

- Because we did it, you can do it to.

Your story works best with a large dose of self-deprecating humor. It is your shortcomings that people relate to, not your strengths. Everyone makes mistakes when they are young. You can set up your lesson by explaining the stupid things you did when you were young. You can explain what you didn't understand and how you learned to do better.

Your personal story leads to your discovery of your "secret formula." You always position yourself as one of the few who have this formula. Repeat the term "formula" or "recipe" or "system" so that your listeners are thinking, "What is that formula he keeps referring to?"

You build your story. Explain how the formula worked in one situation, and then another. Build your story going from one area of success to another. This is how you make the case that it wasn't luck. You make it clear that your good fortune comes down to understanding your formula and applying it.

All this talk of the "formula" sets up the teaching section. You cannot get to the teaching section without setting up the tension of the audience wanting to know what your "formula" is. You do that through your personal story.

The Lessons: Teach a Different Approach

Less teaching is more. In a 90-minute presentation, you serve your audience better by getting them excited about learning more than by trying to teach anything in depth. The more depth you attempt in a limited amount of time, the more you are going to confuse the audience.

No matter how exciting and interesting you make the lesson, the more information that you offer, the less your audience will take away from the experience. You need to teach enough that the audience understands that there is more to learn and that it is well worth learning—no more.

Remember, the purpose of this talk is to get action. Your job is to teach the audience that they need to learn more. If you can teach the audience to do something well in a few minutes, it isn't much of a topic. You can and must create the desire to learn more about your topic.

When I first started giving seminars I tried to teach everything I could in the time allowed. The general impression I created was that strategy was too complicated and deep. Instead of teaching them how to get where they were going faster, I was teaching them how to build a rocket engine. This may have been interesting and even exciting, but it was not practical.

In teaching, you have to explain several key ideas:

1. Why your approach is more complete than any other. Explain, for example, that other approaches use parts of your approach, but they do not work because they are not a complete formula. Without a complete formula, you miss key elements. Without a complete formula, you miss key steps. Other approaches are not wrong. They are just less complete.

2. What the main elements of your approach are and how they work together. Explain the main elements of your approach. You summarize this formula before getting deeper into any aspect of it. You should make this teaching lesson as simple and useful as possible.

In teaching strategy, we introduce people to just three basic ideas: 1) strategy looks at success as a matter of position, for example, positioning yourself as a spokesperson; 2) five factors define every position: the ground, the changing climate, character, methods, and goals; and 3) certain methods are unstoppable in advancing a position, such as making small rather than large steps forward.

3. That there is more to learn but it isn't difficult. Don't be afraid to raise more issues about your topic that you don't have time to explain. You want to raise questions that the audience

might raise, but do not answer those questions. Instead you need to explain that the answers are all there in your system. It isn't difficult because you can make it easy.

4. That there are many rewards to learning your system. You can list all the benefits of the system that you don't have time to get into, but you must make it clear that learning this information just takes a little time. You also need to make it clear that learning this information is important, exciting, and rewarding. Give the audience a list of examples of items that they can learn from studying strategy in greater depth.

For example, you can list the following:

1. Mistakes they will avoid

2. Easy ways to start using your formula

3. Little ways to practice your formula

4. How to minimize making errors

You list these items, giving as many examples as you have time for, but do not explain how you do them—just assert that you can. Give examples of how you use your strategy in business, to advance your career, to make money, to invest, and so on.

Bring It Home

You save your most important, biggest potential benefits for this section. Here, you make the importance of learning your topic more personal. You want to move from talking about the more businesslike lessons to the more personal aspects of life. You must move the talk into a discussion about caring and protecting your

For people to get excited, the lesson section must explain the benefits of mastering a new perspective.

loved ones. You need to put this section in the second person, talking about your audience members and their lives. You go from 100 percent objective teaching to 100 percent subjective, personal value. You put that value in the most personal terms.

For example, in teaching strategy I have said, "Let's say you have a four-year-old daughter and I have a four-year-old daughter. Nothing is more beautiful than a little child, but let's say that unfortunately, our daughters are both sick. Your daughter needs an organ transplant and so does mine. What are you going to do for your daughter? You are probably going to trust your doctor, do what he tells you, and pray. Now, I am going to pray too, but I am going to do more than pray. I am going to use the secrets of being a spokesperson to get that organ for my daughter, and, do you know what? I guarantee that my daughter will have a better chance than yours."

Then you give a real-life example from your own life about how using your topic put you on a different path, made your personal life better, or made you a better person. The purpose is to wind the session down, provide more proof, and create a sense of why your mission is such a passion. The story should put you personally in the best possible light, demonstrating your character.

To connect with people's emotions you have to talk about family life, connecting yours and their own.

You end this part by shifting once more back to the audience members and telling them how their lives will be improved by leaning more about your topic. You just say, "Let me tell you what your life will be like if you master [your topic]." Make it clear that they will still have plenty of problems, but that one area of problems will be solved.

Summary of Three Previous Sections

After making it personal, you summarize what you have taught in the course of the presentation thus far. You mention the grabber you started with and the promises you made about what the audience would learn. You then go through all the mistakes that people make because they misunderstand your topic. You then go through the lessons on what your topic really is and how it works. You then talk about the personal value you can get from mastering these lessons.

The Decision: Get the Audience to Act

This is the last section of the talk. And it is necessarily brief. The essence of sales is speed.

During this last section, you give your audience a powerful incentive to get involved. Everything in the seminar must lead logically to this point. You make it easier for them to move forward and get more from you than for them to do nothing. If you have done your job correctly, most people in your audience now want one thing: they want to know how they can learn more. This section tells them not only how they can learn more, but makes it as easy as possible for them to do so.

You need to accomplish six simple things during this section. First, make it extremely clear what you want the audience to do. Second, give your audience a reason and a way to act immediately. Third, eliminate any fears that keep them from acting. Fourth, give them an opportunity that they cannot get anywhere else. Fifth, give them one more push to help them decide. Finally, give them one last bit of proof that this is the right thing to do.

There are many ways to accomplish these six steps, but a good way to illustrate them is by describing a very specific method I call the "Three Colored Handouts."

Up to this point, you haven't given any handouts to your audience. Earlier they would have distracted from your talk. Now handouts work to get action. When you hand material out, people have to look at it. At this stage, you use this to make your offer tangible and to create action. Psychologically, action leads to action. When you are asking for action, you want to create the feeling that everyone is acting. This method uses a series of three handouts to create flurry of action at the end of your presentation. They are color coded to keep them straight.

Let us call the first handout the yellow sign-up sheet. It is called a sign-up sheet because, if they fill it out and turn it in right away, they get tickets to a special personal coaching session after your speech. This sheet makes it clear what you want the audience to do. To qualify for the special session, people will have to choose what type of action to take. This sheet also offers a clear money-back guarantee so the action is not rash.

Let us call the second handout the blue special offer coupon. This is a half-sheet of paper that offers something more, specially designed for the group you are addressing, that they cannot normally purchase at any other time.

The third handout is the pink testimonial sheet. This sheet lists contains quotes from people who chose to take action about how happy they are that they chose to act. The individuals are selected to be as much as possible like your audience members.

You do pass out these handouts one at a time as part of a deliberate process of using your remaining time productively.

During this process you control the flow of events.

First, refer back to the beginning of your presentation. You remind them of the point you made when you started and what you told them you were going to prove.

Next, you tell your audience that you expect them to act. As the audience gets the yellow sign-up sheet, you spend a few seconds explaining their choices and how making a choice qualifies them for the special offer. If you do a good job of designing your sheet, you do not need to talk about the specifics. You can mention the key differences between the two optional choices.

Then, you emphasize they have a great reason to act now. This is a unique opportunity that they will never get again. A special coaching session is great because it is a one-time event. The deadline is not arbitrary. You are giving the session because you are with them and have a room and the time. If audience members don't act, their chance is gone. This is a logical reason to act now rather than a purely manipulative one.

Especially if you are not immediately delivering the rest of the products, this offer gives people instant gratification. It also appeals to their sense of exclusivity, because most of the audience members will be excluded.

There are other types of strong closings, but the "three handouts" method touches more aspects of persuasion.

Third, you draw their attention to the money-back guarantee. You eliminate the risk in acting now. When you create pressure, you must release that pressure. By asking people to decide now, you create pressure. The guarantee is designed as a release valve. You are so confident in the value that they can get their money back even after the coaching session. The guarantee is written in the biggest print on the sign-up sheet. For example, you can say "If you don't like this offer for any reason, if you don't like the color of packages—send all the materials we give you back at any time and we will refund all your money."

These guarantees are extremely safe. Few people will ever ask for their money back because they see you put in your time and they do get value. It will double or triple your conversion rate, but fewer than one in a hundred will ask for their money back.

Fourth, you make it clear to audience members that they can realize the benefits of this offer only by acting now. You should reemphasize briefly the value of mastering your topic and that your package is the best possible way to achieve that. You also emphasize why the personal coaching session is an important addition. You want to hit the trigger words "secrets," "formulas," and so on. For example, you can say, "As I mentioned earlier, this whole formula and system has been worked out. It has been tested and proven, but there are several aspects that are best learned in person in a smaller group.

Fifth, give your audience a nudge to push them over the edge. At this point, the decision will be balanced in the audience members' minds. To tip the balance, pass out the second sheet. This is a blue special offer coupon on a half-sheet of paper. This should offer an additional product customized for the group that is not normally available at any price—available only to these people today. Again, it is something they lose if they don't act.

> *People always balance every call to action with the costs involved so they always need a little push.*

Sixth, give the audience a crowd to follow. The final sheet, the pink testimonial sheet is technically called "social proof" in the psychology of persuasion. While these sheets are being passed out, you can read some of the testimonials or show videos and play audios. People are more comfortable acting as they see others act. These testimonials are followed immediately by more social proof, seeing other people fill out and hand in their sign-up sheets.

Your Closing

Most people don't know how to stop talking. You must stop talking exactly at the scheduled time, but do not make it sound like you are stopping because of time limits. Don't say, "Well, it looks like I am out of time." This is unprofessional. Instead, right at the end, leave the audience with clear instructions about what you expect them to do next. For example, you can say: "Remember to turn in your yellow flyers and get your invitation to the private bonus coaching session. We are closing the door and starting exactly on time. I hope to see you there."

A Few Final Thoughts on Influence

This presentation format is designed based upon the psychology of influence. I developed the original outline by comparing the presentations given by the most successful speakers line by line. Then I read several books on the psychological research into persuasion and discovered why these speakers were doing similar things in their presentations.

You begin with the end in mind. You have to know what you want the audience to do, which is why you have to think about products before doing a presentation. Like most stories, everything leads logically to the happy ending where your audience acts.

♦ ♦ ♦

CHAPTER 7

NUTS & BOLTS
OF OPERATION

Your Professional Strategy:
From Confusion to Organization

At this point, you probably have more of what you need to start except a little know-how. In this chapter we look at how to set up your office, market your services, book your engagements, and prepare for them. As your operation grows, you need to master a wider variety of tasks and know how to address certain issues that are likely to arise.

Smooth operations are what mark you as a professional. Knowing how to market yourself correctly is the difference between making money and losing money. Fail to prepare correctly for an engagement and you won't get invited back.

Most professional speakers operate out of their homes with little or no staff. You can appear as professional as the most highly paid speakers with a little organization. I started speaking first for my employers and later for my own company, so I just used my business resources to manage my speaking operations. Whether you start within your current organization or not, these tasks are all very manageable.

Your Equipment

A spokesperson requires no real capital, which is one of the things I love about the opportunity. To set up a speaking operation, you initially need only two pieces of equipment that you probably already have, a phone and a laptop computer. The phone is for making bookings. The computer is for doing everything else, including creating your slide presentations.

Your Phone

You can start your business using your house phone or cell. As your organization grows, you will probably get another line for the business—but not necessarily a more expensive business line since you don't need to pay for a listing in the yellow pages. As time goes on, you may want to add a fax line.

The only way you can look like an amateur, or more precisely sound like an amateur, is to answer the phone incorrectly. Answer your phone on first ring. Speak in a caring, friendly manner. Never answer and immediately put the caller on hold. Never ask a caller to call you back. If you don't have time to talk, always take a message, and ask when would be a good time for you to call back. Close with "thank you for calling us" and mean it.

Teach everyone who answers your phone basic phone courtesy. If you are not in to take calls, those who answer must tell callers clearly that you will call back as soon as possible. If the answerer is unable to answer any question, teach them to say, "We will find out and get back to you." This is infinitely more comforting than the typical, "I don't know."

Being a spokesperson requires good communication skills and those skills start with how people perceive you on the phone.

Computer Software

You use your laptop computer for keeping your schedule, correspondence, creating marketing materials, keeping your contact database, and putting together the slide shows for your presentations. All you need in terms of software is Microsoft Office. You can keep your schedule on Outlook. Use Word for correspondence and marketing materials. Keep your contacts in Outlook, Access, or even Excel. PowerPoint is the standard in the industry for preparing and displaying slides for your presentations. You can use FrontPage to develop your web site.

You may eventually want to upgrade to the Adobe products. Photoshop and Illustrator are the standard products for high quality graphics for presentations and marketing materials. InDesign creates professional quality printed material and is essential for designing books. Printers expect to get electronic files in the Adobe Acrobat format. This is known in the industry as the "portable document format." Everyone refers to these as "PDF" files and you have probably seen them on the Internet.

When you start recording your speeches and creating audio or video products, you need a little more software. I tried a lot of audio products until I started using Audacity, which is *Ten years ago, I could not have recommended any specific software but today there are clear standards.* not only the best program I have found for a speaker's needs but is a free web download. I use Intervideo WinDVD Creator for simple video tasks—because it came free on my Windows Media computer—and Adobe Premier for more advanced editing. Of course, you need a writable DVD drive on your computer to produce videos and audio CDs, but that is fairly standard these days.

Presentation Slide Shows

There is a debate among professional speakers and event promoters about whether or not you should use PowerPoint slides. Many of the best speakers believe that any slide show works against the presentation, taking the focus off of the speaker. However, more and more often, if you are speaking above the local unaffiliated or affiliated organization level, PowerPoint slides are expected as part of a professional presentation by event organizers, especially in the corporate world.

I personally am torn on this point. In theory, I agree that slides distract from the speaker. In modern society, we are too used to looking at screens. What makes a speech so powerful is that it is live and intimate. However, I am lazy and very busy. Putting together a slide show in PowerPoint is the easiest way to organize a presentation from existing modules. I create my slides as much for myself as my audience. I tend to ramble if I don't have slides to keep me on track. They also make it easy for me to see where I am in the course of a presentation.

In a recent presentation for the corporate customers of Hyatt Hotels, the organizers said they would use a video camera to put a live close-up of my face on the screen if I didn't use PowerPoint slides. I didn't want to inflict that on my audience. I used the slides.

When you start speaking, this isn't an issue because your presentations are smaller and more intimate, usually in a small banquet room. A few of these organizations may offer a projector, but most will not. In these cases, you can still use your laptop to organize your presentation and keep yourself on track. However, you only steal glances at the screen and never read slides. You concentrate on your audience. In the most profes-

sional venues, you either plug your computer into their display system or transfer your slides, usually via a USB memory drive, to their presentation computer.

In small settings, you can use your keyboard or a wired mouse to change slides. At larger events where you use your computer, you will want to invest in a wireless mouse so you can move around the stage. When using the event's computer, the organizer will provide you with the slide control device.

When you use slide shows, you use them to complement your performance, not steal the show. You want simple, attractive slides. The simpler it is the better. Forget about fancy animation and transitions between slides. Keep everything simple.

The standard text slide is at most six lines of text with not more than six words on each line. Set up the slides so they reveal one line at a time as you speak so the audience doesn't get ahead of you. I personally prefer photographs or graphics that capture ideas more than lines of text because they can evoke emotions. However, graphics are extremely time consuming and expensive to develop. With most of my slide graphics, the first place I go is Microsoft Office Clip Art and Media, which is a free web site with visual content for Office owners.

And be sure to proofread everything. Then proofread it again. Then have a professional proofread it.

Staff Responsibilities

If you start speaking on your own, you are the staff. If you start as a spokesperson for your business, you may need to involve other coworkers or employees. The tasks that need to be tackled are: 1) marketing, which includes sending out materials, making calls, follow-up, and so on; 2) operations, which

includes scheduling events, arranging travel, and so on; and 3) sales, which includes negotiating fees, selling products, billing for sales, shipping, and so on.

As your speaking takes off, you may want to hire someone to take over many of these marketing, operations, and sales functions. As the spokesperson, your job is to act as an expert and authority. Some speakers are comfortable promoting themselves but others are not. If you are shy about self-promotion, you want to get someone with good sales and marketing skills.

Because I didn't personally have the time to speak more than once a month, it didn't make sense to hire someone to promote my services, but it is probably only a matter of time until some smart sales and marketing person joins up with the Institute in that role.

Over decades of speaking, I have met many other speakers at events. The most successful always have someone working regularly to find events for them to speak at. For a good speaker, the marketing role pays for itself in finding more speaking opportunities and more rapid and complete follow-up on the customer funnel. This frees you as the spokesperson from the office, so you have more time to speak, develop products, and work on various forms of public-ity, tasks that only you can perform.

As a spokesper-son, you want to concentrate as much as possible on the type of task that only you can perform.

If you're hiring a marketing person, you want to interview him or her initially on the phone, since the job is 90 percent phone work. When you meet candidates in person, give them some simple instructions as part of the interview ("Pull up a chair. Fill out this form.") to see how well they listen, follow instructions, and if they have

a tendency to argue. Another good test is to ask if they can start right away. Weak candidates will immediately think of problems when confronted with making an immediate decision.

When you hire any operations support person, you want to work side-by-side with them for a period of time until they learn how you want things done. They can eventually work from their home, but most people find it difficult to start a job and really do it well if you don't initially take them out of their house.

There are many other tasks involved with operating as a spokesperson that are easy to contract out. These include developing the graphics, managing the mailing list and bulk mailings, creating marketing material, designing handout material, shipping products, phone response, audiovisual editing, proofreading, and material and product storage.

You can find sources for contract help by asking other speakers, talking to other professionals such as lawyers, accountants, and so on. Your local printer always has some of these types of contacts. You can also place ads. I always use Craigslist because it is free and well read by service providers. Of course, at the Science of Strategy Institute, we recommend our service providers to our trainers.

Like your need for organization, your need for more marketing material grows over time.

Marketing Material

When you first start talking to local organizations, even local small businesses, you do not need any marketing materials beyond business cards, postcards for handwritten notes, and letterhead. You can create these as you need them on your computer and printer. As you advance as a spokesperson, you may want to add other materials.

More marketing materials are not absolutely required. If people are interested in your topic, they will hire you. I speak regularly at large corporate functions, but I really don't have a current brochure. Most meeting planners hear about me from my books and read about me on the web.

A track record and testimonials are more important than a brochure. Event promoters will be wary of bringing you in, even if you are speaking for free, until you develop a list of references. They will be concerned about whether or not you can give good value to their audience. As event promoters, they have a reputation to maintain. Their event is only as good as their speakers. If you are sharing product sales with them, they are also concerned about whether or not you can convert audience members into customers.

Unless you are working with showcases, speakers bureaus, or agents, you do not need an expensive brochure and promotional video. You need material that shows that audiences like you, that you are an expert on your topics, that you are a practiced speaker, and that your topic helps your audience achieve their goals. A brochure and videos are nice to have, but not a must have.

Testimonials

Testimonials—both from audience members and event organizations—are by far your most important pieces of marketing material. Testimonials and client lists outweigh everything else when people are deciding if it will be safe and profitable to invite you to speak.

All testimonials should be as specific as possible. Ideally you

get them in written form, though you can also collect them as recorded audios and videos. Ideally, you want specific comments that could only apply to your unique presentation. You want to get in the habit of discussing getting recommendations before you speak with event organizers.

When you get a compliment, you should say, "I am so honored by your comment. Would it be okay if I quoted you in our materials?" If they agree, say, "Let me drop you a note with that phrasing, just as you said it." Or, if you have a recorder handy, record the audio on the spot. A great way to get audience testimonials is to use rating sheets, a topic we discuss in detail in the next section.

The secrets to getting event organizer testimonials is in your follow-up. When you get these testimonials, always send them a thank-you note. Select and organize your best testimonials. Sort them by venue, industry, specific topic, and so on. This will allow you to select the right testimonial for the right decision-maker.

Your Web Site

You must have a web site to establish yourself as a professional. Web sites have gotten so easy to register and set up that it is a crime not to do so.

Registering a new domain name is fast and easy. You can register your own name, your company's name, or a name related to your topic. You can register them all and have them all point to the same site. You can get hosting for a year for less than it takes to fill up your gas tank.

We own scienceofstrategy.com, artofwarstrategy.com, clearbridge.com, and other names all pointing at our company web

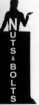

site. We also have seminarsonstrategy.com as a separate site for our trainers. For readers of this book, we have moneyspeaking. com, which offers a wealth of material for speakers available nowhere else.

Your site should contain all your marketing materials. The first version of any material should be a web page. It is easier to develop web pages than printed versions. After your brochure, you add more detailed materials on your topics, your biography, your list of clients, and so on, as you get time to create them. Make sure your web site makes it easy for people to contact you. It should also make it clear what local area you serve.

The Basic Brochure

A simple speaking brochure starts with your topic in big letters across the top. You express your topic in terms of listener benefits. This means you put phrases such as "Win Customers with...," "Make Money with..." "Overcome Depression with..." followed by your topic. After the headline, you put your name in smaller print. You then list the additional benefits of your talk and your qualifications for speaking on it. You add a couple of testimonials, a client list, and a picture of yourself. Finish with your contact information: name, phone number, fax, e-mail, and web site address.

As a spokesperson, you want to concentrate as much as possible on the type of task that only you can perform.

Avoid using blacks, grays, blues, and greens. You want to make materials that can be easily faxed. This means one or two pages. Limit large fields of black or dark colors. Use black and white photos on a light background. Photos should be in low resolution half-tones. You should send

your brochure as a fax to see how it looks.

The digital form of your brochure is more important than its fax form. In its digital form, you can easily customize your brochure for specific markets. You can e-mail it, put it up on web sites, and print it out anywhere when you need it. I use Adobe InDesign and Photoshop to create my marketing materials because they allow more flexible design.

An Event Flyer

The event flyer is a good example of a more complicated marketing piece. It can be created as an on-line page or printed brochure. Designed to promote your own public seminars, a flyer includes a wealth of key elements that can be included in other marketing material.

Seminars are usually advertised "long form," which means that you offer a long, detailed list of benefits, testimonials, bonuses for attending, speakers' qualifications, and so on. In its printed form, the flyer is usually an 11"x 17" sheet printed on both sides and folded in half to make four 8 1/2" x 11" pages. As a self-mailer, it is designed to be folded into thirds with a blank area for mailing information on one of its faces. As an on-line document, it is usually laid out as one, long web page. You do not e-mail the document, but your e-mails give receivers a strong incentive to visit this site and register for the event.

The event flyer is the longest and most detailed piece of marketing material you will ever do.

The flyer should start with a pre-headline with the topic's most important benefit. This is in bigger print and the headline should get attention and again point to the value. Then a post-headline should keep the reader reading into the text.

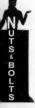

NUTS & BOLTS

The body of the document is frequently written in bullets, with a few short paragraphs of description. Your first section should list your most powerful benefits. You then need a number of testimonials. You follow that with information on the seminar fee and what you get for the money with what-you-will-learn bullets. Then offer attendees a significant early registration discount or bonus. Tell readers who should and should not attend. Then you should give the seminar location and time. Don't forget to tell people that attendance is limited.

On the printed flyer, give readers a registration hot-line number, a web site registration address, a money-back guarantee, and information on cancellations. Make sure you tell readers your qualifications as the seminar leader.

All this information can be reused in a number of other shorter marketing pieces.

Presentation Folders

Presentation folders are a more advanced form of marketing material. They are required by speakers bureaus and speakers agents, but they also add a little credibility when you move into the event and corporate market. These folders strongly resemble a traditional press kit. If you are doing publicity, they share many of the same elements. You do not need all this material to start speaking or even to speak at the highest levels, but it is nice to have, especially if you have someone promoting your speaking services.

These pieces are mailed to event coordinators with a cover letter attached. This letter is on your letterhead. It explains what event the materials are for, what is in your folder, a short summary of your understanding of their needs and how you

can satisfy them, and when you will be calling. The folder itself is either printed, which is expensive, or a standard glossy folder customized with a very nice label or graphic glued to the cover. Inside are pockets for a number of separate pieces.

Among the pieces you can offer are your business card, a one-sheet flyer on a topic that the buyer is expecting, a brochure, a short outline of your presentation, a page on for whom the topic is appropriate, endorsement letters from those who have heard you speak and testimonial quotes scattered everywhere else, a short, one-page biography focusing only on why you are an expert, not your life story, a professional glossy black and white photograph with you in front of an audience, a list of past clients, a mail-back card addressed to you, a product catalogue, reprints of short articles written by you about the topic, reprints of short articles written about you, and audio CD or video DVD demos.

Audio and Video Demos

Audio and video demos are short—usually less than five or ten minutes—examples of you speaking. Of those five minutes, most impressions are formed in the first thirty seconds. Once again, these demos are only required if you are working with speakers bureaus or agents. For others, they are nice to have. In my case, people can and hear see me speak on my web site with short sections taken from our audio and video products.

You usually develop your audio first and then go to video to raise your professional profile. CDs and DVDs are easy to produce in small quantities one at a time on your home computer.

The demonstrations serve three purposes. The main purpose is to show that audiences like you. After that, you want

people to see you know what you are talking about. Finally, you want to show off your speaking ability.

The best demonstrations are not just a few minutes of your speaking. They alternate between speeches before audiences and addressing the potential buyer, describing the services you can perform. A good demo starts with your best segment with a rousing, enthusiastic audience response. You then say something to the buyer about how audiences like you, maybe quoting a testimonial. Then you have another segment of yourself speaking where you make a fascinating point. Then you say something to the buyer about the depth of your expertise. You repeat this process for five or, at the very most, ten minutes. You work in testimonials, speaking products, and biographical credits. If you are using video, you use different live settings. You show the audience and their reactions. You never use canned laughter. You should select unique material that makes you unique. You can easily edit audio to take out the "ums" and "ahhs." You can cut out bad video by cutting to slide or logos of companies for whom you have spoken. Package in bright colors with a color photo of yourself on them.

If you are putting together material for speakers bureaus or agents, do not put your contact information in the content or on DVD or CD labels. They will want to use their own contact information. In the media, you just say, "Please call phone number or send an e-mail to the address on the front of the tape to help achieve the goals of your meeting." If your material channels buyers directly to you instead of through them, agencies and agents will not use it.

Audio and video are going through the same revolution today that print media went through ten years ago.

Marketing

One of the advantages in speaking is that it is itself a great form of marketing. However, before it can work, you need speaking engagements. This is easy at the initial levels of local unaffiliated and affiliated organizations. These first engagements naturally lead to more speaking events at higher levels. When you get your testimonials into the hands of others, your speaking markets itself. It is like a perpetual motion machine once you get it going.

Phone Contact

Getting speaking engagements requires contacting people who host speakers. You already know where to find these organizations from Chapter 5, but you need to schedule time every day to contact them. Initially, you do this by phone. You can then follow up by mailing a letter and any marketing materials. Just making the calls and following up will get you speaking opportunities if you have done a good job of making your topic interesting. If you don't get engagements, ask for feedback about how to improve your topic.

Success as a spokesperson depends as much on follow-up as it does on making presentations.

If you want to be a full-time spokesperson, you need to make up to fifty cold calls every day. There are so many opportunities to speak that this isn't an unreasonable number. There are plenty of events even if you are working only with small organizations within a reasonable drive.

Making Contact Calls

As you call organizations, you first make sure that you are speaking to the person who invites or hires

speakers. If not, you get the contact's name. You then ask what topics are the most interesting to their group. You adapt your topic to the specific interests of the group and ask if they would like to learn more. If it is a paid event or one at which you can sell products, you briefly discuss the money issues (see below). You then find out the date of the group's next meeting. You then send out your follow-up letter and the appropriate marketing materials to those who qualify.

Realistically, you should expect only one in ten of your cold calls to qualify for further follow-up. This means that if you make fifty calls a day, you can get as many ten leads a day. In a short period of time, you will have more leads than you can realistically follow up on.

To follow up, you must contact your qualified people once every speaking cycle. If they have speakers once a week, you follow up once a week. If they have speakers once a month, you follow up once a month. You can set up your contact management system—Outlook or another—so that it reminds you automatically.

As you move up the speaking ladder, especially to professional event promoters, you should even follow up with those who tell you that they aren't interest interested initially. This is especially true if their events seem perfect for your topic. Buyers often routinely say no on the first contact to test how strongly you think you fit with their operation. If you don't follow up, you disqualify yourself. This saves them time and trouble. If you don't give up, you qualify yourself. Those who arrange for speakers often act as an intermediary for higher-ups who can also veto you. If you stay on the event organizer's side and follow up, you will get an opportunity.

How do you stay on the side of meeting planners even when they reject you? Before their event, call them and wish a successful meeting and let them know you can stand in if someone doesn't make it. After their event, contact them and ask how it went. Send them a card to keep in touch.

You should also use their rejection to get a favor from them. Ask rejecting planners if they know some other group to whom they can refer you. When most people reject someone, they usually feel indebted.

You want to leave everyone you talk to with a good feeling about you. You must always speak well of other speakers and other event planners. You want to stay visible, find friends, and try again. Bill Marriot, the founder of the hotel chain, said it best: "Failure? I never encountered it. All I ever met with were temporary setbacks."

Advanced Marketing

Over time, your in-house list of customers and clients is your most important resource. As this list grows, you develop relationships with these people for repeated speaking opportunities. You can also offer past customers bonuses for referring new prospects to you. Following up on past contacts is critical.

If you have additional resources, there are additional types of marketing you can add to the mix over time. They only make sense when you have a full line of products to promote. They are a must if you are promoting your own public seminars.

For advanced marketing, you can look into buying or sharing regular and electronic mailing lists, advertising in third-party newsletters, direct mail flyers, bulk e-mailing to opt-in lists,

advertising in local newspapers and magazines, advertising in trade magazines, getting into business post card advertising packages, and so on.

If you start promoting you own public seminars by mailing out flyers, you have to give yourself enough lead time. This means mailing out your first mailing with a ten- or twelve-week lead time. Many who give these seminars feel mailings work best if you send them out repeatedly, two or three times to the same list.

E-mail is replacing traditional mail, not only because it is less expensive, but because it gets to people so much more quickly. All e-mail promotions are repeated numerous times.

Booking Engagements

When you schedule a presentation, you collect complete information about the event's time, place, and who else to contact regarding the event. If travel is required, check on travel arrangements while the date is being confirmed.

Of course, you must make sure you are available at the required date and time, including travel time. If you are working with others in your organization who are also scheduling your time, you need a method to share your calendar in real time. We upload my calendar to the Internet where others can access it for scheduling publicity and other events. You should be able to schedule at least three years in advance. As you start working nationally and internationally, you need to understand time zones and travel time to schedule correctly.

Keeping a calendar is simple until you have more than one person scheduling your time, then it is challenging.

N
U
T
S
&
B
O
L
T
S

If you have a conflict, you should try to book another date further in the future. You can say, "Let's nail down a time for next [week, month, year] so this won't happen again."

For local unpaid engagements, you need nothing but a verbal okay. You then follow up with your contact on the day before the meeting to make sure nothing has changed.

For engagements that are paid or require expensive travel, you need to get an agreement in writing. Our standard agreement spells out our terms. This includes issues related to taping and reproduction rights, how travel is paid, our ability to get audience feedback, and if we can sell our products. We require a 50 percent deposit 60 days before the engagement to lock in the date and to commit to making travel arrangements. The balance is paid after I speak. You can see a sample agreement at our moneyspeaking.com web site. In some cases, you may want to conduct a pre-engagement interview, described below, before you make an agreement final so that the terms are clear.

Talking Money

You cannot be afraid to talk about the money. As you move up the speaking ladder, money becomes more of an issue. After awhile, you select opportunities based primarily on how much money you can make. Speaking fees are always negotiable, but price is almost always a factor in getting an engagement. As you build up your speaking experience, you find enough opportunities to speak that you must be more selective.

The web site for this book has a wealth of this technical material available for download by book owners.

Some venues will not want you to promote your product or service, so you will need to charge them

a speaking fee. As you begin to question the value of a given speaking opportunity, you start seeking guarantees. You may start speaking for free without guarantees, but you never present yourself as a "free" speaker. You should always ask about the range of fees organizers pay. You may waive or discount your fee or guarantee, but you must always make any discount a limited, one-time offer because of some special circumstances.

Even when you are speaking as a spokesperson for your cause or product, you will eventually require guarantees, especially if an event requires travel. Though you know you can make money from promoting your assets, you cannot know if the event organizer will get a qualified audience to the event. A guarantee assures you that you will get a minimum amount if no one shows up. A guarantee is paid up front by the organizer and he gets it back out of his cut of the sales proceeds before you get your cut.

You can barter speaking fees for free advertising and promotion in a given organization, but you must make sure the event is worthy. Do not devalue yourself and the information you offer by presenting yourself as an amateur. Even if true at that point in your career, it will not help you get speaking engagements in the future.

Your value is based on your past and the client's future. Your speaking experience provides the basis for what you can ask. Value is also based upon how much you can improve your client's future. As you get more experience, you learn you can be of more value to your customers in the future. You increase your fees and guarantee based upon having more knowledge of your market, more contacts, more references, more referrals, and demand for your service. In the beginning, you have to

walk the line between asking too much and devaluing your services. As you keep speaking, you develop a clearer and clearer idea of what you are worth.

You have nothing to lose in asking for fees and marketing opportunities in negotiating an engagement. If an organizer says no, you haven't lost anything. On the contrary, only by asking will you ever receive. Every time you make a contact, you learn more about them and their needs and they learn more about you and the value of the training in strategy that you can provide.

A clear idea of what you are promoting and how you make money from promoting it makes it easier to get engagements. Your message to event organizers and seminar promoters is simple. "I can teach your attendees powerful lessons in a way they will find both valuable and entertaining. At the end of my talk, you and I are going to be splitting a lot of money from product sales. You won't be paying me to speak. I will be paying you."

Whenever possible, you want to talk to the person who is directly responsible for the event, for example, the corporate executives in charge of it. Especially in large corporations, meeting planners are often facilitators and may not be the final decision-makers about who should speak. Going through meeting planners or bureaus can make discussions regarding fees more difficult because they insulate you from all buyers. If you are working through a bureau or agency, remember that they take 25–30 percent of your fee. Renegotiate with bureaus on your fee if you have to work with the client directly to win the engagement.

You can offer buyers a lot of alternative fee structures. For

example, you can have a set fee for a speech, but you might add ten percent if they want reproduction rights for materials. You can add another 25 percent if they want the right to record it for internal use. You can charge 20 percent less if you receive the attendee mailing list. You can charge more if the presentation requires interviews or an analysis. You can add on products. We always offer corporate customers a discount on purchasing our books for their attendees, and they almost always take advantage of the opportunity.

The key to increasing your fees is providing what the client wants. The more testimonials and client references you get, the more valuable you become. Avoid billing by the hour; charge for a project. You should never worry about losing an opportunity. Worry instead about building a customer base. You will make more money if you are willing to walk away from engagements that are not right. Never renegotiate fees, but instead, provide options. Make one option much more expensive and comprehensive than the others to test the buyer's limits.

If you begin with the client's objectives and make clients aware of all your services, you are halfway there. You are not obligated to cite fees early. Start as high as you can. Send your proposals as confirmations of an agreement. Do not accept lower fees to get in the door. Higher fees impress people as providing better quality. Offer the unique aspects of your experience, especially your experience in their industry, as the basis for your fee. Increase your fees if the customer wants you to agree to something inconvenient. Raise fees if you don't like a client.

Being a spokesperson gives you a position of authority from which you can more easily negotiate money matters.

N
U
T
S
&
B
O
L
T
S

Preparing for a Presentation

After you have scheduled an event, you need to start preparing. If travel is involved, you do that first. Then you may want to do client interviews. Finally you can tailor and practice your presentation. Some speakers give the same scripted presentation every time they talk, which requires less preparation. Speakers who get invited back again and again tailor their presentations to the needs of the audience, and have a volume of material from which to draw.

Scheduling Travel

If you are traveling, especially by air, you need to book flights and hotels well in advance of the date to get decent pricing. Note the travel time for the event. You should consider how long it will take you to recover from travel. Never accept a date when there is only one flight available. Never book on the last plane departing before the event. You should also consider potential weather problems, especially flying in winter through airports like Chicago. You should consider travel time from the airport to the hotel or from the hotel to the event. Talk with the meeting organizer and play it safe.

As you become more successful, you travel more and more, which has its advantages and disadvantages.

I always plan at least two nights so I can arrive before the event and get at least a full day to recuperate, meet the event organizers, and prepare. If you are planning on speaking the day you arrive or even the next morning, you will have to carry speaking clothes with you in case your luggage is lost. If you allow twenty-four hours between arrival and speaking, your clothes catch up to you or you have time to buy new ones.

If you are going to sell and deliver products at the event—as opposed to take orders and ship afterward—you need to ship your products out a week before, ideally to the event organizer or the hotel where you will be staying in.

Pre-Presentation Interviews

Your goal is to give both the person that engaged you and your audience the best possible value. This means you have to talk to them in detail before the presentation about what they expect, want, and like. Organizers and audiences don't always have the same interests. I am frequently engaged to give presentations for a corporate customer's clients at a national meeting. Here, I have to meet the needs of the corporate customer, that is, send the right message to their customers. I also have to meet the needs of attendees who are giving up their valuable time to listen to me.

Before the event I talk to a couple of representatives of the group organizing the event, often the event organizer and a corporate executive. I also like to speak to a couple of people representative of the audience. If actual audience members aren't available, the company's salespeople usually have a good idea of the audience interests.

You can spend from a few minutes to an hour or more on these pre-event interviews. I usually spend about forty-five minutes. I ask open ended questions about what they want from the event. I usually wait until a week or two before the event to conduct these interviews. I take notes by hand and then type them up on my computer so I can refresh my memory.

I have a specific set of questions that I ask based upon the key elements of strategy. You can see an example of my pre-pre-

sentation questionnaire at moneyspeaking.com. I always ask about the goals of the event and attendees attending the event. I also always ask about the changes affecting their emotional climate, as we covered in Chapter 2.

You should ask what the organizer and attendees want from this topic. You should ask if they have addressed a similar topic before and when. You should ask what interested them in your topic. Ask if they can offer you specific examples of how your topic might be useful to the audience. I find people are very helpful in giving me good ideas about how I can make my lessons more useful to the audience.

Audience Handouts

Whenever possible, you want to get permission to pass out and collect audience feedback, sign-up, extra custom offer, and testimonial sheets. Feedback sheets are especially important since they are the key to collecting testimonials, improving presentations, finding new leads and turning attendees into customers. You can color code your feedback sheets green so they stand out from handouts.

Getting Feedback

You want your own feedback sheet. The rating sheet used by the event organizers is of limited value. They typically ask audience members to rate each speaker on a one to ten scale based on characteristics such as appearance, delivery style, quality of information, and so on. This is only used to compare you with other speakers at the event, and only the organizers can do this since they see all these rating sheets. Knowing how you compared in these areas to other speakers is interesting but not

very helpful.

The feedback sheet you use is different. I call it the Green Free Prize Sheet to make it clear to audience members that they automatically get a reward for filling it out. The sheet asks open-ended questions and gathers information you can use.

1. What ideas did you hear that you could use?
2. How will those ideas help you improve profits, productivity, and so on?
3. What else would you like to know about this topic that there wasn't time to discuss?
4. Can you think of other organizations that might want to learn about this topic?
5. What is your general opinion of my presentation?
6. Do we have permission to use your feedback?
7. Would you like us to send you a copy of our presentation?
8. How do we get our presentation materials or answers to your questions to you?

You also use this sheet to give audience members a strong incentive to give you their contact information so you can follow up with them. This is the purpose of the last question, but a copy of the presentation and getting their questions answered is not enough.

In big print, you want the sheet to say, "Give this completed sheet to the person collecting them and you will receive a FREE BONUS." You then provide the details of your bonus offer. It should be a product that you don't normally sell. Audience members can get

> *Feedback enables you to improve and it enables you to develop closer and closer relationships with your audience.*

N
U
T
S
&
B
O
L
T
S

it only because they heard you speak as part of this group. Ideally, this bonus is a product that requires no time, cost, or effort on your part. Electronic downloads of audios, additional reports, or your special information are ideal. For example, when you go to money-speaking.com, we offer you a great report PDF on the psychology of persuasion that I did as research for this book along with a number of sample forms. How do you get it? You give us your name, of course. We practice what we preach.

Sales Handouts

In situations where the goal is to make product sales, you can also prepare a sign-up sheet, a special offer sheet, and a testimonial sheet, as we discussed in the last chapter. All three are used at the end of your presentation to close the sale on products.

The Yellow Sign-Up Sheet

The yellow sign-up sheet also offers a bonus. One of the best bonuses is a personal coaching session that takes place soon after your presentation. If you can't get a room for a live presentation, you can make this session a teleseminar. This type of bonus allows you to call this handout a "sign-up sheet" when it is also an order form. The free personal coaching session is a great bonus to give to people who make a commitment to your programs. For example, to give you an incentive to sign up as soon as possible at moneyspeaking.com, we are offering a series of one-time free teleseminars that offer personal coaching on the topics in this book. Your yellow sign-up sheet has five components.

The handouts we described in the last chapter have a very precise format designed to facilitate action.

First, you need a title that is tailored to the audience. For example, if you are talking to the PTA, the title should say, "Training for PTA Members ONLY" at the top.

The next section offers the selection of one or two (or at the most three) product options, minimally a "basic" package and a "premium" package. Under each package, you list the various components that make up the product, the regular "retail" value of those individual items, the total value for each, and the discount you get for ordering them as a package. There is a clear checkbox by each allowing the user to select the options they prefer.

Then, the nature of the free bonus session is printed in a larger font and says something like: "Give this completed sheet to the person collecting them and you will receive a FREE TICKET to a private strategy coaching session at [TIME]. The location of that session will be in your tickets."

The fourth section allows them to give you their mailing and billing information.

Finally, you offer a written money-back guarantee that says that they can get their money back, before or after they get delivery if they are unhappy for any reason.

The Blue Bonus Coupon

This is an additional incentive to buy now but one that only makes sense for those who buy your products from the yellow sheet. Ideally, this bonus is another product that requires no time, effort, or product costs on your part, but it is tailored to the audience and something that the audience cannot normally purchase.

The design is simple. This coupon should only be a half-sheet of paper. The coupon title should be tailored to the audience. Put the bonus offer in terms where they only qualify for it if they act immediately.

The Pink Testimonial Sheet

These are regular people's testimonials selected especially for the group you are addressing. These are customers who not only heard you speak, but bought your product. They are selected on the basis of how closely they and their needs resemble the group you are addressing.

Tailoring Your Presentation

Most speakers tailor their presentation to one degree or another for the specific group they are addressing. At first, you are creating your presentation from scratch. As you get more experienced, you have more material than you need. You have to select what you want. In every situation, you want to give your listeners the best possible experience for the money.

I usually spend from an hour to three hours selecting and customizing slides for a presentation. As I go through my basic material on strategy, I review my notes about the organizer's and audience's interests to select the appropriate slides. I use examples based upon these interviews to create new slides. For example, to illustrate the importance of adapting to changes, I might create a slide that lists the major changes affecting their organization or industry and discuss what they mean strategically.

I then create the opening and closing for my speech. In these sections, I address the most emotional and spiritual aspects of the organization's mission. I may use stories from my own life to illustrate how their missions affect me personally. For example, when I recently addressed the Hyatt group, I used "The Problem Story" opening to tell about arriving in Paris in the middle of the night to my hotel room cancelled.

When you finish your presentation, make a backup onto a disk or a memory drive. If you can save a second version that is backward compatible to older versions of PowerPoint, do so. Carry your backups with you, but separate from your computer case. If your computer is stolen or malfunctions, you can use your backups on another computer and give your presentation.

Rehearsing Your Presentation

How much rehearsal you do depends on how comfortable you are with your material. Some rehearsal is usually necessary depending on how much you have customized your material.

You first rehearse your presentation to make sure you can end exactly on time. Nothing is more embarrassing than being cut short or, worse, finishing with time to spare. You cut out or add material to get the timing just right. Identify the slides that represent your timing benchmarks so you can know if you are running ahead or behind schedule as you present. I usually know the slides that are milestones for the first quarter, first half, first three quarters, and last tenth of my presentation.

Once you get the timing right, you may want to rehearse your opening and ending and any emotional high points. I usually work from a day or so right up to the time of the presentation working on these key components.

Remember, no presentation is going to be perfect. Nor is your presentation important in the big scheme of things. If you take a sincere interest in the audience's needs, people are usually very kind. You cannot worry about the rare exceptions.

The more often you speak, the more polished your presentation becomes and the better you get at reusing parts.

N U T S & B O L T S

Other Advance Arrangements

You also want to know in advance who is going to introduce you, who is speaking before and after you, when the breaks are, and if you can get space and time for a special session.

Especially at larger events, you must make sure you are introduced correctly. A good introduction is essential to getting you off to the right start. You can write out an introduction, but the best introductions are given from the heart.

Do not wait until the seminar to find out who will be introducing you and make contact with them. Before the seminar, take time to bond with the person who will introduce you. Make an impression as to what a great person you are. You don't just want an introduction; you want a personal endorsement. Insist that you are introduced by the seminar organizer or someone else known to the audience. An introduction by the audio visual guy or the room monitor doesn't give you any credibility. The best person has a financial incentive to make you look good.

You should know when you will speak, how long you will speak and who will speak before and after you. You should try to get out of any spots right after cocktail hour. Ideally, you want to be the first speaker of the day.

The more loose ends you can wrap up before, the less you have to worry about on the day you speak.

The time to schedule breaks is before the presentation. You should not take a break during the presentation if it is shorter than two hours. However, you cannot go three hours without taking a break. You want to limit breaks during a presentation to ten minutes. Ideally, they should appear on the seminar schedule. The person who announces you should mention them as well.

If you are selling products at the event and offering a bonus coaching session, you should make arrangements to get a time and place for space before the seminar. You must get a break right after you speak so you can work the audience. The ideal place to sell products is in the back of the room or just outside, ideally on the path to refreshments or the bathroom.

The bonus session can be in any room that the event has already booked. You just need to get a time when it isn't busy. This is often during a meal break or after the last session of the day.

A Final Thought on the Nuts and Bolts

The devil is often in the details. This chapter represents a detailed checklist for building your operations into the future. When the time comes where you have to tackle one of these tasks, such as designing your brochure, you can always refer back to this chapter to do it correctly.

Avoid reinventing the wheel whenever possible. When you need to address a new area of operations, it is always easier to ask advice from a few people with experience than to try to figure it out yourself.

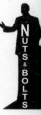

—Chapter 8—

Game Plan
for a Great Day

Your Event Strategy:
From Setup to Sales

This brings us at last to game day. You are going to speak. You are prepared to speak, but you still have some work to do before, during, and right after your presentation. In this chapter, we address the technical details of making the speech pay off that cannot be addressed before the event.

Your first presentations to small groups do not require much of this work. But as you move up to bigger and bigger events, you need to know how to prepare the room, prevent technical problems, avoid common mistakes while you are speaking, collect feedback and testimonials, and interact with attendees before and after the event.

As you hit your stride as a spokesperson, you become more confident in your talk. This allows you to focus on the purpose of the event and get the result you desire. For events at which you can make sales, we also cover the critical issue of how you take orders in the smoothest, most effortless way possible.

Before the Seminar

Most of the issues we address here are important for more advanced presentations, but many of them are less important in smaller presentations. The idea is to avoid problems that will detract from your presentation. You are setting the stage for everything to go perfectly.

Meet With Organizers

You need to meet with the event organizers. First, you need to meet with the person introducing. Then, you need access to the meeting room so you can check out the equipment, seating, lighting, and so on. Then you need to work out details of passing out and collecting information, setting up an autograph table, and arranging the private session room. You may also need volunteers assigned to help you with various tasks and schedule a meeting with them before your session to give them some simple training.

You especially want to meet who is introducing you and have him or her get to know you. However, you don't want to tell too much about the actual context of your presentation beforehand so he or she cannot give away your big lines.

Meet With Attendees

It is a good idea to meet with a few attendees before you present and, if possible, see other presentations before yours. This allows you to further tailor your presentation to the audience's interests.

If attendees ask you about your presentation or your products at the beginning of the

The attendees are your prospective customers; you want to charm them at every opportunity.

GAME PLAN

day with just a few people around, give a very brief description of what you do. Offer to tell them more with the whole group.

If people ask questions right before with lots of people around, just tell them you will give a complete description during your presentation. It is especially unprofessional to pitch your products right before talking.

Getting to the Room

Knowing the seating arrangement, lighting, temperature, and projection system can only help. Sometimes you cannot adjust these factors, but often you can if you can get access to the room before the presentation. As a general rule, you want to get into the room as soon as possible to identify and eliminate potential problems.

You also want access to the room right before you speak to test your slides. If you haven't made arrangements to pass out your feedback sheets—green prize sheets— after you speak, take this opportunity to put them on every chair right before.

The Projector

Minimally, you must test the projection system for your show before you present. This means hooking up your computer or getting your slides on their computer. Though PCs and PowerPoint have become the norm, you can still run into problems. I have had several situations where we had to get a new projector before the show because the one initially provided didn't work.

Like the soft-ware, the equipment has become more standardized and easier to operate than ever before.

This equipment is often provided by the convention center or a rental agency. They are

just bringing it to the room and plugging it in. They don't necessarily turn it on, see if it is aimed at the screen, or hook it up correctly. I have often had to play around with the projectors to figure out how to get computer output up on the screen. Don't expect local people to know. If no one can get it to work, you don't need to project your slides. Just use your laptop as your teleprompter to keep you on track.

One time, I couldn't get my computer to work at all because the projection system required some software installed on the computer, but I had a backup of my show on disk (now I use a USB memory stick) that I installed on one of their presentation computers. If you have to move to a different computer, go through a few slides to make sure it is working. Unfortunately in my case, the computer had an older version of PowerPoint that couldn't handle my animations. I didn't find out about these problems until I started the presentation for the audience.

Don't repeat my mistake. Make your slides simple and test any new system going through a few of your more complex slides to see what happens.

Make sure you have all of your equipment. Bring your power supply. Don't trust your laptop batteries to last, even if they should theoretically.

Lighting

You want as much light in the room as possible and still see the screen. Most projectors allow you to have some lighting. If you have to dim the lights to see the slides, see if you can get someone who can raise and lower the lights for you. Some rooms have remote controls for the lights. You want to find them and learn how to use them.

Your audience must see you. You must be the show, not the slides. At the end of the show, the audience must trust you, believe you, and want more of you. The audience needs to see your face. You want them to see your expressions and body language. If you are going to bond with the audience, they have to see you. If you have to choose between showing your PowerPoint presentation and the audience seeing you, choose to be seen. You must never work in the dark. A voice coming out of the darkness doesn't win anyone over. The ideal environment is one where you have a light directly on you, but the light doesn't shine on the screen. In the best presentation rooms, you have a spotlight on you. This makes it hard to see the audience, but it does make you the center of attention, which is what you want.

For a long training session, you may have periods of low light when you are showing slides, but most of your time must be spent in full light, talking with one another and interacting. Otherwise you are going to lose your audience.

Seating Arrangements

Some speakers consider seating arrangements to be critical for a presentation, but in my experience just about any seating works if you are prepared for the room. Every type of seating arrangement suggests a different presentation style. However, you want to know—if not control—the seating arrangement before the show, so that you can plan accordingly.

In theater type arrangements—no tables, seats in rows, next to each other—you get the best audience attention. However, do not suggest that the audience take notes at any point in the show because taking notes is difficult without tables. In a classroom environment, where people have desks in front of

them, you can tell them that they should be taking notes now. You want to give them note taking assignments so they don't use their note pads to work on other projects.

In a dinner room environment, where people are seated around tables, I will use fewer slides or go without slides at all. Any speaking opportunity is good, but it is hard to speak while people are actually eating. Try to speak after the meal or before rather than during. In dinner environments, you entertain more and educate less. After a dinner, especially if there is drinking, I prefer to make my points with jokes and stories, never with bullets. You focus purely on exciting the audience about the topic. Again, make it clear they won't have to take notes.

Arranging the Room

If you have control over the room, choose theater seating with the chairs arranged in a semi-circle. Semi-circular and straight theater style seating have the audience sitting close together. Because they are close together, you get more audience reaction because reactions tend to pass from one person to other. People touch each other and glance from side to side at each others' reactions.

When you arrange the chairs in a curve, audience members can look to their left or right and see the faces of other people down the row. Mood is contagious. These environments work extremely well if you can put some humor in your presentation. People laugh just because they see others laughing. As the presenter, you want to get the audience involved and see that others are enjoying the presentation too. This is a form of

While you cannot usually control the seating arrangements, you should know what seating works the best.

G
A
M
E

P
L
A
N

social proof. People take their cues from seeing others.

Semi-circular seating is also more comfortable because people don't have to turn their heads to look toward the presenter. This is much better than straight theater style where the audience members at the end of a row must turn their heads sharply to see the presentation. This creates an uncomfortable audience member in a very short time. An uncomfortable audience member is less likely to get involved. Do whatever it takes to keep your audience comfortable and involved.

Those in charge of room set-up don't like semi-circular seating because it is more work, but they will do it if they are required to. If the room is small and you get to the room early enough, you can often make changes yourself. Remember, your job is to please the audience, not the set-up crew. If the presentation doesn't go well, the audience blames you. They won't ever blame the set-up people.

If chairs are fixed or there isn't room to set chairs in a semi-circle, you need to be more animated and move around more. This allows attendees to move their heads to see you, thus creating more interaction and increasing the chance they will see each other's reactions.

Another trick in fixed seating theater arrangements is to ask the audience to choose a new seat after they come back from a break. This can give them a whole new perspective on the presentation and tends to get the more interested people up front where they can better interact. When you do this, you must tell the audience why you are doing it—to change people's perceptions— and you must give the instructions before the audience takes a break.

When you start hosting your own seminars, choosing the right seating arrangements are particularly important.

People are very territorial. They instinctually think that they own their seat. You'll upset them if you take away a seat they own for no reason so you must tell them how important it is to change their perspective.

Keep Close to the Audience

Get as close as you can to the audience when making your presentation. Distance between you and your audience creates a barrier. If the environment allows you to walk out into the audience, take advantage of it. You never want to get trapped into giving your presentation behind a podium if you can avoid it.

I put my computer where I can see the screen and still get as close as possible to the audience. I hate being tethered by a corded mouse to the computer because I prefer to move, pacing the front of the room.

You want people to sit as close to you as possible in the front of the room. This is not the natural tendency. In most rooms, the back will fill up first. Ideally, you want the person managing the room to direct the audience to the front rows. As people file in, you, your announcer, or a room monitor can ask them to move forward.

You can even force the audience to the front with reserved signs in the back or on back tables. You can also keep chairs stacked until existing rows are filled.

If the room is narrow and deep, see if you can set up the presentation along the long wall, with the seats curving around. That way, you have few rows in the audience and can move back and forth to make up for the long wall. In a long, deep seating arrangement, when you are way up in a narrow front, too much of the audience is too far away. You want the room to have as

many aisles as possible.

People want to sit next to an aisle and not get trapped in a row. This is especially important in rooms with wide rows. People will sit near the aisle, blocking others from the middle of the row. The rule is that no person should ever have to cross more than six other people to get to a seat, but even that is a lot.

Also, no chairs should ever be put next to the walls. If an aisle doesn't run down the wall, the audience members feel trapped.

Technically, aisles should get wider as they get near the exits because they must accommodate more people. You also want to get into the aisles to interact with audience members.

The Room Temperature

If the room is too hot or cold, people cannot listen to you. As the room fills up, body heat warms the room, so the empty room should feel a little cool before hand, but not cold. If at all possible, see if temperature adjustments can be made during the presentation. Make sure someone is assigned before the presentation to make adjustments and knows how to make them.

If you can't get the temperature right, you must acknowledge the audience's discomfort during your presentation. You can sympathize, make jokes about it, work it into your presentation as a lesson, and encourage everyone to make the best of it. Your indifference or insensitivity is more damaging than the uncomfortable room itself. This is a lesson from strategy: it doesn't matter what the environment throws at you. It is how you react that matters.

The Sound System

If people cannot hear, they won't listen. This isn't a problem in small rooms, but in big rooms, even if you are close to the audience, it never hurts to use a sound system. This is especially important if you get people laughing. You must be heard over the audience reactions. An entertaining presentation demands a better sound system than a serious talk. In a serious talk, words can be missed, but the message is still understood. When using humor, missing a single key word can ruin a joke or story.

If you get to the room early right before your presentation, you might be able to do the sound check. It usually takes a couple of minutes to get a good sound level and you don't want to do it in front of the audience. Again, in an empty room, a good level will sound a little loud because people absorb the sound once they get into the room.

You never want a microphone for the audience. You do not want to take questions during the presentation. You want to control the only microphone and have it either in your hand or on your lapel. When you control the microphone, you control the room.

Recording the Presentation

You should record every presentation you make, both so you can critique yourself and so you can make products and marketing material out of the result. If the event organizers are recording the event, get a copy. Sometimes, even if they aren't recording, the sound people can. Get the recording right afterward. It is always

Even in smaller groups, a sound system is useful if only because it allows you to easily record your presentation.

GAME PLAN

extremely difficult to get recordings from others later on.

If you are doing your own recording, check your recording equipment beforehand. Make sure the batteries are fresh and charged and that you have enough tape. Make arrangements with someone to change the tape if necessary.

During the Presentation

We examined the parts of a great presentation in great detail in Chapter 6. Here, we offer some important rules you should keep in mind whenever you speak, whatever format you use. Your goal isn't just looking good or training the audience. It is being a spokesperson and making money, which means you have to concentrate on two key issues: First, you want to create an experience where everyone wants more. Second, you want to turn an anonymous audience into customers.

Control the Time

Do not lose track of time. You must start on time, stay on time, and, especially, end on time. The key is getting started on time. Let audience members know how long you will be speaking, and what they will get from listening.

If there are breaks, you want to prepare your audience so they know how long they have to wait. This is common courtesy. If people know when a break is coming, they are able to relax and concentrate on the presentation instead of worrying about their bladder. You discuss them not in the very beginning, but after you have the audience's interest.

You always call your breaks "ten-minute breaks," or "five-minute breaks," depending

When you are speaking, take charge of the room because too often no one else is going to take responsibility.

GAME PLAN

on the size of the audience, but they will always take longer. You never tell people that they have fifteen or twenty minutes, because they will then get involved in activities that could take a half hour. A five- or ten-minute break gives people some incentive to get their coffee, relieve themselves, and get back as quickly as they can.

Toward the end of the break, stand outside the meeting room and say loudly, "He is starting! He is starting."

Control the Audience

You must pay attention to the audience's reactions. You cannot just keep talking without keeping the audience involved. You test and measure your audience every five or ten minutes by asking for a response from them. You can ask for agreement from the audience ("Can I hear an 'Amen'?"), ask an easy question to the whole audience ("Has anyone here ever had problems making up their mind? Can I see hands?"), or make a little joke.

Never ask for volunteers from the audience or announce that you are going to single out an individual. When you say "I am going to ask for a volunteer," you create tension in the room. Everyone starts worrying about getting called upon and they stop reacting. To get individuals involved, just walk up to them and ask them directly what you want them to do. For example, hand them a card and say, "Would you read this?"

Don't pass out notes or handouts before you speak. They give people a reason not to listen. You tell people when to take notes depending on the situation. "From now on I just want to see the tops of your heads because you're going to be busy taking notes." Or even better, you tell them materials will be

available afterward if they give you contact information. You then collect their business card or contact information so you can mail or e-mail it to them. This gets their names into your sales system.

You cannot let other people take the floor during your speech. Do silence an interrupter. You're being rude to the audience when you let someone else dominate the conversation. You can say, "I have the microphone and these people are here to learn. If you want to be the speaker, you should offer your own presentation."

Control the Value

You should not give out products to the audience because it discourages the receiver from buying something because they already have something. Do reward people answering questions or making contributions but make rewards small things like candy.

Avoid saying anything that discourages people from wanting more information ("This is where it gets hard.") Don't give any information that doesn't lead to a sale ("You might think this is expensive..."). Talk about the value of all the information that you don't have time to give them ("There are a lot of easy techniques you can master for..., but we don't have time to discuss them all now.").

You cannot separate yourself as a spokesperson from the product you are speaking for. Actively build yourself up in subtle ways, name special tricks or techniques after yourself. Rivet your name and your brand image into people's minds. Make yourself a part of the brand.

You cannot pretend to be someone that you are not. Use

whatever personal assets or defects you have—your look, your handicaps, your personal problems, your personal success—to your advantage. Make them a part of your presentation.

You cannot ignore the real world problems of the group or organization that is in trouble. Instead, give groups that are in trouble a solution. "You are going to suffer more if you don't do something else, and I am here to talk about the solution not the problem."

You must use testimonials over and over. Weave your testimonials into the presentation with stories. For example, say, "The last time I spoke to this group, this person used my approach and did this..."

Follow the format in Chapter 6 as closely as possible; excite the audience about what you offer and leave them wanting more. You can attack conventional wisdom and competitors by name. Make the audience understand the lifetime value of what you offer, but don't pitch the products directly. Focus on the benefits of what your products do for others. You should love your products, but readily admit that they aren't going to make them automatically successful without their contribution.

Don't forget to make people an irresistible offer that gets them to act at the end. In sales situations, this offer is built around your products and filling out your order sheet. In situations where you are not selling, the close is built around getting the audience to return your feedback sheet. Minimally, you must instruct everyone why they want to fill out these sheets and the bonuses they get for filling them out.

Usually, you will leave no time for questions,

The end of your presentation is about your offer, not about other questions that were raised in the presentation.

GAME PLAN

so you ask the audience to put any questions on the feedback sheets, so you can answer them either after the session or through e-mail.

If you are not using feedback sheets, do not forget to ask for testimonials and references from every group you speak to and from every customer you sell to. Ask for that audience's help in finding more audiences and more customers.

Do not show your forms and sheets on the screen or walk the audience through how to fill it on the screen. Make any sheets self-explanatory and give audiences time to fill them out. You want people filling out the form, not looking at the screen.

After the Presentation

Only after your presentation can you make money. There are a number of issues you need to address.

The Order Break

When you set up your speaking engagement, you should insist on a 15-minute break after the talk so people have time to turn in their sheets. If you are using sheets to collect feedback or orders, you have time to get those sheets. If you have anyone helping you collect sheets, it is best to make one person and only one person responsible for getting them all together.

After talking, your work shifts to helping the audience give back to you, whether you are collecting feed-back or orders.

During the order break, you should stay in the front of the room, or in the middle of the center aisle, where you are approachable, and leave your microphone on. You should take compliments from people on your talk so that everyone can hear. If people ask you general questions about your topic or offer, answer

them for the whole audience to hear. Answer their questions fully and completely. Give people a lot of great information and never withhold information to get someone to buy your product.

Some of the questions are very helpful. For example, you want to answer on the microphone, "Yes, we take American Express."

People will approach you with questions. In return for answering questions, always ask people for something in return, for example, to fill out a feedback sheet. If you don't have a feedback sheet, ask the people you talk to after the event for feedback, references, and testimonials. Avoid using the phrase, "Can I have..." when asking for something from someone, like a testimonial. Instead, ask them, "How can I get..."

If someone tries to get into a specific topic that will take a long time to explain, you want to delay answering until after the order break.

At some point, if people are filling out sign-up sheets say to the audience, "Remember if you don't print carefully, things won't be shipped correctly, it won't be delivered and it will come back to us because we couldn't read it."

While waiting, give autographs if people ask.

If people are still coming up when the next speaker is ready to speak, take people to the side or out of the room. You can say, "Folks, come over here." Move toward your product table if you have one or out in the hall if you don't. You want to clear the room as a courtesy to the next speaker.

After the Break

Get copies of all the feedback or order forms from the people who were collecting them. Stand by the coffee and refreshments

reading the sheets. This will give others more opportunities to approach you. After the break between speech and coaching sessions, stay in the general area to get more orders. As much as 20 percent of your orders can come from making contact with audience members after your session.

If people come up to you and say that they are going to take advantage of your offer later, you should tell them sympathetically that they won't. Life has too many distractions. You should firmly tell these people for their own good that they need to commit now or they never will. Otherwise your presentation will be just another opportunity that got away.

Working the Product/Autograph Table

If you have a product sales table at the event, you can call it an autograph table especially if offering books you can sign. Bring in a limited amount of inventory to create scarcity. Take orders when your inventory is gone.

People want instant gratification, but they don't need all of what they order. If you can deliver just part of your product package, for example, a single book, CD, or piece of software, people will be glad to wait for the rest. If you are offering a bonus coaching session, that alone can satisfy those who order.

You should not try to process credit cards after a show. It slows sales down. People will not wait in line. You will lose more sales to impatience than bad cards. People should be able to fill out order forms while they wait in the line. Your helpers can then just check to see if the information is complete and give receipts and any products.

If you are taking orders, you will need help working the sales table after your presentation. Audience members will

want to talk to you. In local presentations this isn't a problem, but when you travel, you need to get volunteers locally or hire temps.

Follow Up With Event Planners

Usually, it is difficult to meet with the event planners after you speak at the event. You may be done, but they are still in the middle of the event. When the event is over, they want to relax. If you can get together, you want to sit with them and review your best feedback sheets. If possible, you want to book their next event on the spot. If you can't get together with them, copy and send feedback forms to send to them. Then call to book future engagements.

A Few Final Thoughts on the Game Plan

The temptation is to be so focused on your presentation that you lose sight of the larger goal. Before the event, you can be too distracted to think about preparing the right environment and making a good impression on attendees. During your presentation, it is more important to make the audience comfortable and get them motivated than it is to get through your material. After your speech, you can be so relieved you let everything else go, missing out on the best time to get orders and bookings.

The solution is to be well-enough rehearsed that, by the day of the event, you can take care of all the details that avoid disaster and secure success. You can then work through your before, during, and after checklist and let the actual presentation take care of itself. ♦ ♦ ♦

A Time to Act:
$297 Package Free

To demonstrate how valuable the methods in this book are, I want to give you an irresistible reason to start using them today. Go to your computer right now. Sit down and go to www.moneyspeaking.com.

Free Package for Spokespeople

For a limited time when you visit the Money Speaking web site, you will see a green link called Free Package for Book Owners. Click on that link and you will be prompted for a key word you will know from a specific page in this book. This will give you access to our exclusive book owners' area.

In our book owners' area, you can download our Money Speakers Starter Kit, which includes sample PowerPoint shows, illustrating ideas from this book and audios demonstrating ideas such as real life examples of the different types of openings. It also includes a number of the forms, questionnaires, and other materials for speakers we describe in this book. One of the most valuable products is our exclusive research report on the psychology of influence that explains various psychological triggers on which this book's methods are based.

Sign Up for a Free Personal Coaching Session

After the publication of this book, I will be hosting a series of personal coaching sessions. They will cover the various topics in this book: making your life story interesting, developing a valuable form of expertise, creating assets, and so on. During this coaching session we will offer those who join our advice about what works and what doesn't and why.

Click on the link highlighted in yellow to learn how you can qualify to take part in one of these live sessions, but hurry. We will only be offering these live sessions once. Each one has a limited number of spots. Those who sign up first will be given priority in terms of getting their questions answered. The sooner you sign up, the better.

A Few Final Thoughts on Making Money

By this point, you should be seeing the possibilities in your current position in a very different light. It doesn't matter what your life experiences have been thus far. It doesn't matter what your job is currently. It doesn't matter what your goals for the future are. You should now understand how the spokesperson strategy offers you a shortcut to success.

The time to act is now if you want to break away from the herd and begin a real life adventure. Follow the thousands of people before you who have used these techniques to stand up, get themselves heard, and start producing the type of value that always leads to making more and more money.

Before you read this book, you had an excuse to settle for less in your life. Now, you have no excuse because you know the best way to pursue your dreams.

The Science of Strategy Institute
WWW.SCIENCEOFSTRATEGY.COM

BOOK PROGRAMS
Library Memberships
Book Clubs
Books and Audios

ON-LINE TRAINING PROGRAMS
The Warrior Class
The Strategy School

ACADEMY OF STRATEGY
On-line Training
The Academy Library
Mentoring on Life Strategy

STRATEGY INSTITUTE SEMINARS
A Worldwide Network of Trainers
Internal Corporate Licensing

About the Author

Gary Gagliardi is the founder of the Science of Strategy Institute. He is the award-winning author of over a dozen books on strategy. In 2006, he won the Ben Franklin Award for the best psychology/self-help book. After building one of the Inc. 500 fastest-growing companies in America, he has gone on to train the world's largest organizations in the principles of strategy. Visit **www.scienceofstrategy. com** to learn more about his books and programs.